101

SCHOLARSHIP APPLICATIONS

101 SCHOLARSHIP APPLICATIONS

What it Takes to Obtain a Debt-Free College Education

2019 Edition

Gwen Richardson

FIRST EDITION

Cover design by Cory Wright

ISBN: 978-1793814845

10 9 8 7 6 5 4 3 2 1

Printed in the United States of America

To my daughter, Sylvia,
who inspired me to go the extra mile

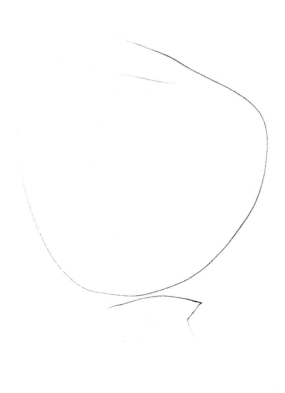

TABLE OF CONTENTS

INTRODUCTION

We have all read headlines featuring a fortunate college-bound student who has received $100,000 or more in scholarship awards. Assuming that the scholarships were renewable annually, this amount could easily pay for four years of college at any American college or university. As of September 2017, the cost to attend Harvard University, one of the nation's most expensive and prestigious institutions of higher learning, was about $64,000.[1]

However, these success stories, while inspiring, are the exception, not the rule. They are aberrations among the pool of millions of aspiring college students who submit scholarship applications to the hundreds of companies, foundations, and non-profit groups that offer them. The reality is a much different, and sobering, picture. According to leading scholarship experts, the average 2016 undergraduate who borrowed money to pay for college graduated with about $37,000 in student loan debt.[2] In addition, there are more than 44 million college loan borrowers with $1.3 trillion in student loan debt in the United States alone.[3]

Three years before our daughter, Sylvia, was headed for college, we began researching scholarship sources and believed that we were well ahead of the game. We purchased the book titled *Peterson's Scholarships, Grants and Prizes,* a mammoth reference tool of nearly one thousand pages. I personally spent a dozen hours combing through the different sections of the book for scholarships that applied specifically to her field of study (accounting), her state of residence (Texas), and her ethnicity (African-American). Using a highlighter and sticky note tabs as referencing tools, I thought I was well-prepared for the task that lay ahead. Little did I know that the landscape that lay before us would be quite different than we expected.

Scholarships Are Highly Competitive

Our biggest surprise was the level of competitiveness of the scholarships that are offered. The competitiveness of the college application process is well documented and, at many colleges, 10 percent or fewer of the applicants are admitted. The 2018 pool of applicants to Harvard University, for example, was 42,749, with only 1,962 students – or 4.59 percent, who were admitted.[4] The scholarship process is more competitive by far.

Conversely, the Fifth Third Bank Scholarship received 3,600 applicants for its 2017 award of $2,500 to 28 student winners. This is a ratio of less than 1 percent.[5]

Other scholarship organizations report similar results. The FedEx Scholarship, administered by the United Negro College Fund (UNCF), received 1,600 applications for only five scholarships, an award ratio of less than 1 percent.

Cast a Wide Net/Apply For *Lots* of Scholarships

With that level of competition, a student must cast a wide net to have a reasonable chance of winning enough scholarships to cover most, if not all, college expenses. That was the impetus behind my choice for this book's title, *101 Scholarship Applications*. Even though our daughter had an exemplary high school academic record -- a GPA of 3.8 on a 4.0 scale, in the top 9 percent of her graduating class, and 300 hours of community service during her high school years

-- we had submitted our *seventy-third* scholarship application before we received our first award letter for her freshman year of college.

The letter we received was for a scholarship that had been submitted several months prior to that, but the important thing is that we did not become discouraged during the process. At that point, we had already received about 20 letters of denial or regret, which was a bit disheartening, to say the least. But we continued to submit applications until we started receiving positive results.

With the combination of grants and scholarships, at about the time she moved into her college dormitory for her freshman year at North Carolina Central University, a historically black college/university (HBCU), her entire year's expenses were paid in full. Some of the financial aid was renewable annually as long as she maintained a GPA of 3.0 or better. She graduated four years later with absolutely no student loan debt.

Yet, not only will the volume of scholarship applications increase a student's odds of winning, but the exercise itself has merits. As you prepare dozens of submissions, you will hone your skills and your applications will become more and more refined. You will begin to see patterns in the process, which will allow you to anticipate what selection committees expect. And you will begin to accumulate the materials needed, making the process less challenging as the months progress.

Myths About Scholarships

There are several myths about scholarships that will be dispelled in this book.

Myth #1: Only students with high GPAs qualify for scholarships. In actuality, eligibility requirements range from 2.5 to 3.5, with an average of about 3.0. Many scholarships do not require a minimum GPA and are based on other factors, such as community service or an essay competition. In addition, although a limited number of scholarship applications require the inclusion of SAT scores, the scores are primarily utilized for the purposes of confirming that the student took the test. It is rare that a scholarship will have a requirement of a minimum SAT or ACT score.

Myth #2: Only students from low-income households can obtain scholarships. While many scholarships are based on financial need, there are many others that do not take family income into consideration during the process.

Myth #3: Most scholarships are awarded to students from ethnic minority groups. There are many scholarships that are specific to students who are African-American, Hispanic or Asian. However, there are many more scholarships for which ethnicity plays no role regarding eligibility.

Myth #4: Most scholarships are limited exclusively to high school seniors. A student's senior year in high school tends to be when most individuals begin pursuing scholarships, but scholarship funding is available throughout all four years of undergraduate study, as well as during graduate school. In fact, among the scholarships listed in this book, only 20 percent are restricted exclusively to high school seniors. Most are for undergraduates at any level, and about 10 percent are available to students at the graduate level.

Myth #5: The student should be solely responsible for the scholarship application process. A generation ago, the scholarship process was relatively simple. Once a student received acceptance to a college or university, the institution sent a statement reflecting the financial aid for which the student qualified. The statement would include Federal grant programs, school-based financial aid, student loans, and work-study programs. The student simply accepted the financial aid package and everything was handled through the institution.

That is no longer the case. Because the cost of a college education has skyrocketed over the past two decades, colleges usually do not offer enough financial aid to cover all of the expenses, even for those students who qualify. Colleges still send financial aid award letters to those students who meet their eligibility requirements. But individual award letters may include a higher percentage of student loans than scholarships and/or grants, including the Parent Plus loans for a student's parents.

If a student seeks to reduce these expenses by submitting multiple scholarship applications to a variety of sponsoring entities, the amount of time required will be substantial. During high school junior and senior years, students who are high academic achievers will take advanced placement courses in calculus, chemistry, physics, English, and a foreign language, requiring them to spend a significant number of hours in course work and study. The same is true for college students. Participation in extracurricular activities, community service projects, and part-time jobs will also be time-consuming. Most students simply will not have enough hours available in their school day to perform all of the work required for scholarship submissions.

Parental assistance will be required to perform necessary tasks, including, but not limited to, the following:

- Ensuring that all scholarship deadlines are met,
- Retrieving, copying, or scanning necessary documents,
- Editing essays prior to submission,
- Requesting letters of recommendation from teachers and advisers,
- Visiting the high school registrar's office or contacting the college's registrar's office to request official transcripts,
- Following up with scholarship organizations that request additional documents,
- Making sure that any documents the educational institution must complete and submit to the sponsoring organization are completed and submitted by the required deadline,
- Making sure the scholarship funds actually arrive at the financial aid office and are applied to the student's account,
- Contacting scholarship organizations whose websites experience technical difficulties,
- Contacting scholarship organizations whose award checks are for the incorrect amount (this actually happened to us),
- Double-checking scholarship packages to ensure all documents are included prior to mailing or online uploading, and

- Traveling to the post office to mail scholarship packages or other required documents.

Myth #6: A debt-free college education is no longer possible. Based on a January 3, 2018 article in *College Campus Life News* this myth has become widespread. "It's almost unheard of for someone to finance their undergraduate education themselves or through scholarships," writes Lorena Roberts, a reporter for the online publication.[6]

However, a debt-free college education *is* possible. There are a number of factors involved, such as the dollar amount the college charges for tuition and fees; whether the institution is a private one or a public one; whether or not the student attends college in a different state, thus incurring out-of-state fees; the student's declared major; and the amount of effort the student and his/her parents are willing to expend when identifying and applying for scholarships.

The purpose of this book is to assist parents and their college-bound children with the scholarship process and sources for awards. It is information that I wish I had when I first embarked upon my quest for a debt-free college education for our daughter.

It is my and my husband's belief that, once a student graduates from college with a bachelor's degree, he/she should be able to launch a career without being saddled with a mountain of debt that is the equivalent of a mortgage. With the compound interest, penalties and fees assessed, a college loan debt of $40,000 or more can take decades to repay, especially if the individual experiences any periods of unemployment throughout his or her career. In fact, many college loans are now structured with a 25-year payout schedule! Outstanding loan debt in the six-figure range is not uncommon, especially for graduate students.

The days of an individual working for one company for 40 years without interruption are virtually gone for good. This increases the likelihood that, at some time along one's career path, there will be at least one period of unemployment. Our hope is that those who read this book will be able to avoid mounds of college loan debt, and begin their professional lives with a clean financial slate and a favorable credit score.

College students and their parents will most likely experience pressure to borrow money for college – from the institution the student attends, from former students who have debt, and even from family members. If students resist the pressure and eliminate or minimize college loan debt, they will experience the delayed gratification of being debt-free when they graduate.

After conducting several years of research and spending hundreds of hours on the scholarship application process, compiling all of the information into a book seemed appropriate. Once you achieve success by utilizing the tips and strategies included in this book, send an email to me at gwenrichardson123@gmail.com and let me know when your goals have been achieved. I have also created a Facebook page (https://www.facebook.com/debtfreecollegebook) where I post new scholarship opportunities, photos, pertinent news articles, and scholarship success stories.

CHAPTER 1

DEVELOP A PLAN OF ACTION

Before getting started with the scholarship application process, you will need to know the most important factor involved. The answer might surprise you.

In fact, the most important factor is not the student's grade point average, SAT score, or resume; nor is it the level of objectivity among the members of the selection committee, or the comprehensiveness of the scholarship list used as a reference tool. While these factors do play a meaningful role, they are not the most crucial. The most important factor is the level of commitment parents and students bring to the task.

High school students must be committed to putting forth their best effort in their school work; to taking both the PSAT and the SAT tests twice; to participating in appropriate extracurricular activities and community service projects to enhance their academic portfolios; and to associating with other equally-driven, like-minded students who are also preparing for college matriculation. College students must be committed to utilizing effect time management during their course study; maintaining high GPAs; and becoming involved in campus and community activities.

Parents must be committed to motivating and encouraging their children (the students); to conducting much of the research required to identify the scholarships; to performing much of the required leg-work; and to maintaining a continuous, positive attitude, even after the rejection letters begin to arrive. Without the commitment, success will be elusive. But it is better to potentially spend hundreds of hours of diligent work on the front end to secure scholarships for a debt-free college education, than to spend 30+ years repaying the principal and interest on a five- or six-figure college indebtedness.

Cost of College Education

Now, here is some background information on the cost of obtaining a college education. College costs have increased at a rate much higher than the rate of inflation over the past 20 years. The median household income rose by 20.3 percent between 2002 and 2012, the most recent year from which data is available, according to the U.S. Census Bureau. By comparison, during the same ten-year period, the College Board reports that the average cost of tuition, fees, and room and board for an in-state student at a public four-year university rose by 66 percent.[7]

As a result of tuition hikes, educational borrowing has also increased dramatically. According to the New York Federal Reserve, the average 2016 college graduate had $37,172 in student loan debt, and more than 43 million Americans are encumbered with student loan debt.[8] In years past, educational borrowing was once capped by law at $4,000 per family per year. But the amount of student loan debt is now unlimited.[9]

High School Performance Is Important During All Four Years

As with any project or goal, developing a plan of action is the first step. The quest for college scholarships actually starts in the student's ninth-grade year of high school. Students should take the PSAT in both grades 9 and 10 (some students take it in the eighth grade), and the SAT in both grades 11 and 12. The more practice students receive taking these critical exams, the higher their scores will be. There are several books that can be purchased that include sample test questions and students are encouraged to obtain one or more for review purposes. One of the best known books is *The Official SAT Guide*, published by the College Board.

Cumulative grade point averages (GPAs) are assessed from ninth to twelfth grade and every semester counts toward the class rank and overall GPA. Enrolling in either advanced placement (AP) or dual-credit courses while in high school will boost a student's GPA and class rank, if the student receives a grade of C or above. Thus, it is highly recommended that students enroll in at least two or three advanced courses each high school year. Enrollment in advanced courses will help distinguish you from those students who do not, and provide you with an advantage during the selection process.

In addition, preparing more completely for college by taking AP, honors and additional math and science courses in high school tends to result in increased college completion rates. Several studies have shown that completing rigorous academic curricula in high school may also help students overcome a variety of socioeconomic disadvantages.[10]

Some scholarships, such as the Dell Scholars Program, require participation in specific academic programs during both the eleventh and twelfth grades.

If you are a high school junior or senior, you may not have taken the above information into account during your freshman and sophomore years. However, you still have enough time to make adjustments to your curriculum, extracurricular activities, and community service projects.

Regarding the actual scholarship quest, you will need to begin work on your scholarship project at least 12 months in advance of college matriculation, preferably during your junior year of high school. Starting early will give you an opportunity to fully develop your initial database of scholarship opportunities. As you work on your applications, you will identify dozens more along the way, some of which you will decide are too time-consuming, complex, or competitive to pursue.

As stated previously, applicants should be well aware that the pursuit of scholarships is a highly competitive process. Millions of students from across the United States, many of whom are in the top ranks of their graduating classes, will be pursuing the same pool of limited scholarships.

Yet, the competitive nature of the process should not be a deterrent. By submitting dozens of scholarship applications, you can increase the odds that you will receive a few awards of differing amounts. After all, depending upon the scholarship funding level, five or six awards could be enough to pay all of your direct college expenses. Therefore, be sure not to ignore scholarship opportunities that appear to be relatively small – in the $500 to $1,000 range. Applications for the smaller amounts tend to be less cumbersome to complete, and several small scholarships combined can add up to a large amount overall.

Some of the largest scholarship awards come from the colleges and universities themselves. If you have already submitted your college application, or are an undergraduate presently enrolled, the college financial aid office will be the best source for starting your scholarship quest, but they assign and disburse those funds early.

When a university offers a package that is described as a "full ride," many do not include room and board in the package. Room and board costs $7,000 to $10,000 or more per year, depending on the campus. Be sure to ask what's included in the "full ride."

It is a good idea to become acquainted with the head of the institution's financial aid office. Make regular contact with him or her to inquire about new scholarship funds that may have become available. Some students forgo funds because they decide not to accept admission to the institution, or because they receive outside scholarship funding that exceeds their college expenses. These funds are then made available to other needy students. Also, new financial aid funds for students are received by the institution throughout the year. Developing relationships with members of the campus financial aid office staff will keep the student plugged in for any new funding opportunities that arise.

Finally, the initial financial aid award letter you receive from the college of your choice will probably include student loans. However, you are not required to immediately accept the loans. After you receive your scholarship award letters and you are aware of your remaining outstanding balance for the academic year, you can always apply for a college loan then, if necessary.

Influence of Social Media

The influence of social media has become widespread over the past several years and the scholarship process is not immune from the prominence that sites like Facebook, Twitter, and Instagram play in the lives of college-bound students. A number of scholarships include a social media component to the application process. Some of the social media techniques include:

- Requiring applicants to "like" a sponsoring organization's Facebook page,
- Making the popularity of a social media post a factor in advancing applicants to the next level of the competition,
- Writing 140-character tweets on a specific topic, and
- Posting the scholarship award recipients on the sponsoring organization's Facebook page.

The Dr. Pepper Tuition Giveaway (listed in Chapter 9), for example, requires that applicants create Facebook posts on which the page's fans will vote. Once an applicant has received at least 50 votes, he or she will become eligible to submit a video in the next level of the competition.

As a reflection of the importance of social media in assessing an individual's credibility, some scholarship organizations actually request links to the applicant's social media pages. In other words, sponsoring organizations do not want to be blindsided by awarding a scholarship to someone who may ultimately embarrass the organization because of inappropriate social media posts.

In the coming years, as the popularity of social media continues to increase, more and more organizations will include a social media component in their scholarship application requirements.

Set a Goal

Before beginning your research regarding the various scholarship opportunities that are available, decide what your ultimate goal will be in terms of a dollar amount of scholarship awards. If your goal is to cover all of your college expenses for at least the first school year, then be sure to tally all the applicable costs, including tuition and fees, room and board, and books. The vast majority of scholarships submit the funds directly to the educational institution, referencing the student as the recipient. There are, however, a few scholarships that provide the funds directly to the student to cover related expenses, such as the purchase of a laptop, living expenses, or travel expenses.

There are a sizeable number of scholarships that are only awarded in the sophomore or subsequent years of college and not available to college freshmen. If the student is a graduating high school senior who will be matriculating to college in the upcoming fall, scholarship applications for future years should be maintained separately for submission in later years. Once you complete your first round of scholarship applications for freshman year, you may find that future funds are not needed. This would be a good problem to have!

If you are getting a late start and are already attending college, you still have the opportunity to complete the remainder of your college years without student loan debt. As stated above, there are many scholarships that are available to students during all four years of college, and even some for a fifth year of undergraduate work.

A second step in the planning process is determining how many hours per day or per week you will spend researching scholarship opportunities and submitting applications. As stated previously, in order for this quest to be successful, the student and/or his or her parents must be committed to a consistent regimen.

While working on my daughter's scholarship project, I spent about two hours per day on weekdays, for a total of about 10 hours per week, for at least eight months during her senior year in high school. I believe this is the average amount of time required because of the tedious nature of the work involved. It is a data-driven exercise and also requires an attention to detail and a high level of organizational skills. The amount of time spent continued during her college years to ensure she remained debt-free, although by junior and senior years I was able to cut the amount of time in half.

Since the student's time will be consumed with involvement in academic assignments, community service projects, extracurricular activities, part-time jobs, and preparation for prom and graduation during senior year, I highly recommend that the parent(s) take the lead on the scholarship project. It will allow for the student to submit applications to many more sponsoring organizations than the student could accomplish on his/her own.

Basic information about the student has to be entered repeatedly on both online and paper applications, and it is *not* required that the student personally complete these. The vast majority of scholarship applications are either online forms requiring document uploads, or the documents must be submitted to a specified email address. The essays *are* required to be the student's own work, but parents can help there, too, with editing and refining the finished product.

Finally, you must determine the different avenues that you will utilize for your informational sources. Reference books on scholarship opportunities are a good starting point. But also inquire with your school's guidance counselor, browse websites specializing in scholarships (these will be discussed in detail in Chapter 5), obtain word-of-mouth information from other parents, contact local organizations that offer scholarships, and, most importantly, contact the financial aid office of the intended educational institution once the student has received an acceptance letter. Inquiries via all of these avenues should be made periodically (at least once per month) since new scholarship opportunities are regularly announced to the public.

CHAPTER 2

BE ORGANIZED

As mentioned in Chapter 1, a high level of organization will be required to successfully pursue your scholarship project. Without it, you will not have all of the required documents to accompany your scholarship application, or you will miss scholarship deadlines, resulting in lost opportunities to compete for funds.

The most important aspect of your organizational process is the deadline date for each scholarship. Your data should be placed in order by date with the most imminent deadline at the front of the pile, and then going forward thereafter. Scholarship deadlines are strict; applications are not accepted after the deadline and organizations make no exceptions for late submissions.

For online applications, pay close attention to the time and time zone of the deadline, as well as the date. It is best to submit your application several days in advance of the deadline and not procrastinate until the last minute. However, there may be some instances in which you do not learn about a scholarship until a few days before the submission deadline. The deadline for online submissions is usually midnight, but the time zone could be Eastern, Central, or Pacific. Double and triple check deadline times and dates since, once the deadline passes, your opportunity will have gone with it.

In addition, pay close attention to the eligibility requirements. Some scholarships are only for graduating high school seniors, while others are for those already enrolled in college. Some are for a specific major or have a minimum GPA. Others have a state residency requirement or are restricted to specific educational institutions.

There are a variety of methods one can utilize to maintain the information about potential scholarship opportunities. Some use the spreadsheet method, listing each of the scholarships in an Excel file with separate columns for all of the pertinent information. When my scholarship quest first began, I attempted to use this method. But I quickly discovered that the spreadsheet was inadequate for the voluminous information needed to stay abreast of each program and its requirements.

Instead, I opted for the traditional file folder system, creating a file folder for each scholarship with a label on the tab. When I found information online about the scholarship, I printed the instructions and/or the application and put them in the folder. Email communications were printed and included, and letters received or sent via snail mail were also included.

In addition, I used a Post-it note on the front of each folder, listing the deadline date, the sponsoring organization, and the documents required for submission. As each document was acquired, it was placed in the folder and scratched off the list, until all documents were obtained. Using this system, I always knew which documents were outstanding, and I was constantly aware of the looming submission deadline.

I did, however, create an Excel file to alphabetically list each scholarship application which we completed and submitted, along with the award amount, deadline date and submission date. I did this to avoid duplicating effort and creating files for scholarships for which we had already applied.

Most scholarships require all documents to be submitted online and uploaded to the sponsoring organization's website, or forwarded via email. A small but sizeable percentage of scholarships require that all documents be submitted via U.S. mail. For those that are mailed, usually the package must be *postmarked* by the deadline date, but sometimes the package must be *received* by the deadline date. Make sure you include the distinction between the two in your notations. Allow at least two weeks for packages to arrive via snail mail, unless you pay for expedited delivery via FedEx, UPS or the U.S. Postal Service with a guaranteed delivery date.

There are also scholarships that give applicants the option of submitting packages either online *or* via U.S. mail, but these tend to be relatively few in number.

For online applications, if recommendation letters are required, the entire process is automated. The sponsoring organization will require that the recommender complete and submit the form on the scholarship web site. The applicant submits the name and email address of the individual(s) who will submit the recommendation, and that person receives a direct email notification.

However, teachers and counselors will often have dozens of students requesting recommendations and the deadlines can easily slip through the cracks. I found this to be one of the most challenging aspects of the online submission process. Recommenders must be respectfully nudged along during the process, since they have no incentive to fit these tasks into their schedule other than their willingness to assist the student. Checking the scholarship submission website daily, only to see that the last recommendation form must be submitted before the application is concerned to be complete, can be frustrating.

It is the applicant's responsibility to make the requests early (at least two weeks before the deadline), and follow up with the recommender to ensure that forms are submitted on time. Develop a list of individuals who are willing to be recommenders and spread the work around to avoid overburdening one or two people. Ask at least double the amount required. Avoid the sheer disappointment of having all of your documents submitted on time, yet having the organization reject the application simply because one recommender forgot to submit his or her online form.

Develop a Team of Recommenders

As college students and parents pursue scholarships, it is very important to develop a team of reliable recommenders that you can call on in a pinch. You should never wait until the last minute to submit applications or notify teachers, community service mentors or employers that recommendation letters are needed. But many scholarships now require the entire process to be completed online, which means recommenders actually have to create an account, log on, and submit the recommendation on the sponsoring organization's website. If the recommender fails to follow through, the application will be null and void even if all other parts of the application have been completed.

We actually had a crisis like this during the summer before our daughter's sophomore year in college where a recommender failed to complete the process and was on vacation as the deadline loomed large. Because we had a team of recommenders -- people who were invested in our daughter's college success -- we were able to call on one of them to complete the process and he came through. (By the way, our daughter actually won that scholarship so having the team of recommenders is extremely important.) When there are thousands of dollars at stake, one mistake can mean the difference between college loan debt and a debt-free college education.

CHAPTER 3

REVIEW RESPONSES TO
FREQUENTLY ASKED QUESTIONS
ABOUT THE SCHOLARSHIP PROCESS

After you have conducted your research and submitted your scholarship applications, the waiting begins. But, before you get started, be aware of the responses to the following frequently asked questions.

How much time does it take to complete a scholarship application?

The amount of time required varies widely from one scholarship opportunity to another. A few scholarship applications take 30 minutes or less to complete, although these are definitely in the minority. Others take several hours or days as information may need to be gathered from a variety of sources and signatures obtained. Be prepared to spend at least two hours completing each scholarship application.

Am I required to pay an application fee for a scholarship?

A few non-profit organizations require that an application or processing fee be paid, but these requests tend to be rare for legitimate scholarships. There are some organization's that require a student to be a member in order to apply for scholarships, which means the annual membership fee must be paid prior to submitting an application. Before paying the membership fee, be sure the organization is reputable and actually dispenses scholarship funds to students each year.

If an individual or company requires you to pay a finder's fee for a scholarship search, this is usually a red flag for a scam. Be leery about individuals or companies who want to serve as middlemen between you and your scholarship funding or who claim to guarantee a scholarship award. No third party can guarantee that a student will receive a scholarship award.

You may receive solicitations from organizations requesting that you pay a membership fee, after which you will become "eligible" for college scholarships. These solicitations are usually scams, designed to prompt you to pay the membership fee, but the scholarships never or rarely materialize.

In addition, beware of "informational" seminars that claim to provide expertise on college financial aid. Although some of these can be legitimate, be aware that they tend to offer few specifics, and are primarily designed to serve as vehicles to pitch high-priced scholarship services.[11]

How long will it be before I am notified about the scholarship award?

The length of time each organization takes to notify scholarship applicants of their decision varies widely from one sponsor to another. In general, the length of time is directly related to the complexity of the application, the number of applicants, and the number of accompanying documents required.

Scholarships that are based solely on an essay will usually make a decision within about 30 days after the deadline. For others with more complex packages, a decision is usually made within 60 days after the deadline. However, many scholarships take much longer – four to five months is not uncommon.

About half of the positive scholarship award notifications for which we applied did not arrive until after fall college classes had already begun. If the student has a letter in hand announcing that he or she is a recipient of an award, the college admissions or registrar's office will usually accept this as an official notification that the funds are forthcoming.

How will I be notified of the selection committee's decision?

The method of notification depends upon the organization, as each organization is different. In general, these are the methods of communication:

- By telephone, followed by a formal letter via snail mail or email,
- By email,
- By snail mail, or
- No notification at all

In some instances, the selection process will go through several rounds. There will be a group of finalists selected and a telephone or in-person interview is conducted before the final decision is made.

Many of the sponsoring organizations only make direct contact with those who receive awards. For these organizations, their websites will usually indicate an expected date when the award is to be announced. If you do not hear from the organization by that date, assume that you are not an award recipient. If a sponsoring group does not indicate a specified announcement date, visit the group's website periodically. Usually, the award recipients are posted there or on their Facebook page.

Receiving rejection letters and emails is part of the process of submitting scholarship applications, but reading these communications is never an enjoyable experience. Yet, with the number of applications you will need to submit to achieve your goal of a debt-free college education, you will receive dozens of letters that begin with "Thank you for submitting your scholarship application. We regret to inform you. . ." You must take all of this in stride and not let these letters discourage nor deter you from your primary objective.

Does the sponsoring organization explain why I did not receive the scholarship?

Unfortunately, no. The organization does not usually provide an explanation, other than to state that there was a lot of competition for only a few slots. The decisions of selection committees are final and are not subject to appeal. However, you have nothing to lose by writing a letter or sending an email requesting feedback, which could be helpful especially if you plan to reapply in the future.

What happens if my scholarship funding exceeds the amount due to the school in tuition, fees, room, board and books?

If the student already has financial aid in place to cover all expenses, the institution may reduce the funding of some school-sponsored grants and scholarships if additional scholarship funds are rewarded. Remember: The vast majority of scholarship checks (about 90 percent) are made payable directly to the institution and funds are sent to the school's financial aid office. Some scholarships will require the student to certify that there is still unmet financial need before forwarding the payment to the school. If all college fees have been paid in full, the scholarship may be awarded to another student who has outstanding financial obligations.

If a student has received a Federal Pell Grant, the amount of funding is usually the same each year as long as the student maintains a specified minimum GPA and the family's financial resources have not dramatically changed.

If the student has already acquired student loans that have been applied to the student's school account, the institution may issue a refund check directly to the student for the amount in excess of tuition, fees, and room and board. Policies differ from one institution to another, so it is best to check with the college financial aid office for clarification regarding excess funds.

For those scholarships where the funds are awarded directly to the student, these funds may be retained by the student for books and other school-related expenses, as long as this is permitted based on the scholarship guidelines.

Do I need to submit 100+ applications every year of college matriculation?

The number of applications submitted depends upon how much time the parent and student devote to the process. For the first two years of our daughter's college matriculation, we submitted close to 100 applications. However, for both the junior and senior years, we found that the award amounts increased within her discipline (accounting), and the requirements were more precise. This meant that the level of competition was not as great and her award percentage increased.

For her junior year we submitted 40 applications and by senior year the number was down to only 25. The funds for the entire academic year were received earlier. For junior year, all funds were received by January of the spring semester. For senior year, all funds were received by August before the academic year began. Both years her scholarship award dollars actually exceeded the maximum amount her university could accept for her expenses. For junior and senior years, the GPA requirements for scholarships tend to be 3.0 or greater so the student will need to keep that in mind to maintain a debt-free status throughout the college years.

Are there strings attached to scholarship awards?

Many corporations provide scholarships to students as a way of giving back to their local communities, or to maintain reputations as good global citizens, or to groom future potential employees within their industries, or simply because it is good public relations to do so. As a general rule, scholarships do not have strings attached to them in terms of the student having to claim fealty to a particular political philosophy or corporate identity.

If a scholarship is renewable, the student may be required to maintain a minimum GPA. A few scholarships will require students to attend a leadership conference, serve as mentors to future scholarship recipients, or participate in an internship program. The vast majority of scholarships, however, do not require that the student perform any activities after the scholarship has been awarded.

Are scholarship funds taxable?

Scholarship funds are *not* taxable if they are used to pay for tuition and fees (books, supplies and equipment) for course work for individuals who are candidates for degrees at a college or university. Scholarship funds *are* taxable if they are stipends, or are used to pay for room and board.[12]

However, a student claimed as a dependent can receive a yearly income up to $6,300 (as of 2016) without owing federal income tax. This should cover at least one semester of room and board at most institutions. For students who are not claimed as dependents, a yearly income up to $10,350 can be earned without owing federal income tax.

For Pell Grants and other Title IV need-based education grants, they are tax free as long as they are used for qualified education expenses (as stated above) during the period for which a grant is awarded. Borrowers of federal and private education loans may deduct up to $2,500 in interest as an above-the-line exclusion from income, even if the taxpayer does not itemize. Please keep these stipulations in mind regarding filing tax returns and reporting income.

CHAPTER 4

COLLECT THE REQUIRED DOCUMENTS

Scholarship applications require a variety of supporting documents, some of which will be requested for the majority of package submissions. Some documents are requested less often, depending on the needs of the organization. It is very important that the information included in the documents is accurate and truthful, since inaccurate or false responses are grounds for immediate elimination from the process. For some scholarships, the submission of false information, if discovered prior to the dispersal of funds, can result in the scholarship award being rescinded.

After spending several years submitting hundreds of scholarship applications, I have compiled a comprehensive listing of the documents that were required. The most commonly requested items are listed first.

- Applicant's personal information (legal name, permanent address, phone number, email address, date of birth, social security number)

- Information about applicant's high school (name of school, address, phone number, email address, fax number, principal's name, guidance counselor's name and email address), or college

- Information about applicant's parents (both parents' names, address, phone numbers, email addresses, social security numbers, places of employment, job titles, educational attainment, income)

- Applicant's school performance (dates of attendance, class rank, number of graduates in class, GPA, courses taken, grades in each course).

- Applicant's transcript (Official transcripts must be submitted directly from the educational institution. Some scholarships accept unofficial transcripts, with official ones needed only if applicant is awarded the scholarship or is a finalist.)

- Applicant's SAT or ACT scores (official printout from College Board showing date(s) taken and scores in critical reading, math and writing). PDF format of scores is required for some online applications. The majority of scholarships do *not* include SAT/ACT scores as one of their eligibility requirements.

- Applicant's resume, listing career objective, employment record, honors and awards, extracurricular activities, and community service projects. A one-page resume is preferred. Continue to update the resume as the student's career advances and/or evolves.

- Copy of parents' tax returns for the preceding tax year, being sure to blackout social security numbers (Some applications require tax returns for multiple years, but this is rare.)

- Student's digital photo, usually a head-and-shoulder shot of student only. Some scholarships require submission of an actual glossy photo via snail mail.

- Copy of applicant's birth certificate, passport or naturalization papers (for proof of U.S. citizenship)

- Copy of FAFSA Student Aid Report (SAR) indicating expected family contribution (EFC) (explained in more detail in Chapter 6)

- Copy of college acceptance letter; address and phone number of institution

- Contact name, address and phone number for financial aid and/or admissions office at college which student plans to attend

- Federal school codes for the institution(s) to which student has been accepted

- Recommendation letters from teachers, counselors, advisors, or other individuals who can assess the student's overall performance. Most scholarships require at least two recommendations, but it is suggested that five be obtained to cover all contingencies. Each year, you will need to receive updated recommendation letters from instructors at the student's existing educational institution to maintain current items within your records. (Note: Recommendation letters from relatives are not allowed. Some organizations require that the letters be in separate, sealed envelopes.)

- Names, email addresses, and phone numbers of individuals who submit recommendations (required for some applications submitted entirely online)

- Certification of community service hours expended during high school or college. Some scholarships include pre-printed forms that must be completed; some require a letter from a leader of the organization for which hours were performed; others require online submission of certification.

- Applicant's personal statement, about 250 words in length. This is the basic essay that introduces the student to the sponsoring organization and includes information about family background, school performance, extracurricular activities, career goals, community service activities, and the reason why student is applying for the scholarship. (More information about the all-important essay is included in Chapter 7.)

Make sure that all documents are in clean, smudge-free condition, accurate and factually correct. Elicit the assistance of an English teacher or trained editor to review the student's personal statement to ensure it is grammatically correct, succinct, and error-free.

CHAPTER 5

VISIT IMPORTANT ONLINE
SCHOLARSHIP SOURCES

There are many websites that offer assistance with scholarship identification and acquisition. The best scholarship websites have updated information and regularly post new scholarship opportunities. During the years we spent researching and pursuing scholarships, the following were the ones we found to be the most comprehensive and helpful:

Cappex.com (www.cappex.com) describes itself as "your college decision headquarters," the place to discover new colleges and scholarships, compare your top choices and make the decisions that give you peace of mind. Students create a log-in account and enter basic information so scholarship opportunities can be efficiently matched.

Chegg.com (www.chegg.com). Based on its comprehensive student profile, Chegg.com can match students to over $1 billion in scholarships and merit aid awards. Students tell Chegg.com who they are, and the site hooks them up with scholarships that matter, as well as college and graduate school information. The site also offers a college textbook rental service.

The **College Board** (www.collegeboard.org) is a mission-driven not-for-profit organization that connects students to college success and opportunity. The College

Board administers the SAT and Advanced Placement testing programs, but its web site also lists scholarship opportunities.

Fastweb.com (www.fastweb.com) is the premier online resource for paying and preparing for college. Fastweb members are matched to relevant scholarship opportunities completely free of charge. With roughly 1.5 million scholarships worth more than $3.4 billion, there are scholarships for *every* student's educational goals, activities and interests. Students create a log-in account and enter basic information so scholarship opportunities can be matched efficiently.

Fastweb.com also publishes interesting articles that include information that is relevant for college students.

You may remember seeing Chris Gray, creator of the **Scholly** phone app (www.myscholly.com), during his appearance on ABC's "Shark Tank." Gray landed a deal from investors Daymond John and Lori Greiner and, since then, Scholly has grown to be one of the top apps in both the iOS App Store and the Google Play Store. The company was named in Inc. Magazine's Top College Start Ups, won Under Armour's Cupid's Cup competition, and won Steve Case's Rise of the Rest Competition. Gray was named Ernst and Young's Entrepreneur of the year for 2015 for Philadelphia and is one of Forbes' 30 under 30 for 2016.

The team of scholarship researchers at **ScholarshipExperts.com** (www.scholarshipexperts.com) has created a successful data management and research process. The company believes that the accuracy of the records housed in its award database is the cornerstone upon which its service is built, and works year-round to maintain accurate award information. The team works closely with scholarship providers to ensure that students using the site receive current and accurate scholarship information–and the scholarships in its database have been submitted or verified by the actual award providers.

The information at **Studentscholarshipsearch.com** (www.studentscholarshipsearch.com) is based on a program created by the Edvisors network that provides an organized platform for students to search, investigate, and apply for scholarships. The website helps students find scholarships that are most relevant to their background, field of study, sport, skill, interest, achievement, or other attribute.

Thurgood Marshall College Fund (TMCF) (www.tmcf.org) is one of the nation's largest organizations exclusively representing the Black college community. To date the organization has awarded more than $250 million in such assistance to its students and member-schools. TMCF distributes 98 percent of its awards exclusively to HBCUs and Black colleges.

The **United Negro College Fund (UNCF)** (www.uncf.org) is the nation's largest and most effective minority education organization. Since its founding in 1944, UNCF has raised more than $3.6 billion to help more than 430,000 students receive college degrees at UNCF-member institutions and with UNCF scholarships. Students create a log-in account and enter basic information so scholarship opportunities can be efficiently matched. The website only lists scholarships that are actively accepting applications, so check about once monthly to see which new ones have been listed.

CHAPTER 6

UNDERSTAND THE IMPORTANCE OF THE FAFSA SCORE

The Free Application for Federal Student Aid, also known as FAFSA, is the vehicle through which the Federal government determines which students receive Federal financial aid in the form of grants, loans, and work study. Administered by the U.S. Department of Education, FAFSA is also the yardstick by which most college financial aid offices and several sponsoring organizations determine which students should receive financial aid, as well as the appropriate amount. It is an essential part of the scholarship application process.[13]

The FAFSA application is available online each year after January 1, and should be completed by the student or parent as soon as possible thereafter. Completing and submitting the application is free and quick, and gives students access to the largest source of financial aid to pay for college, vocational school, or graduate school.

Beginning in the academic year 2017-2018, the U.S. Department of Education implemented a change in the way FAFSA is submitted. Students are able to file their FAFSA applications as early as October 1 for the following academic year. This means they will no longer have to wait for their W-2s to arrive before they get started, and can get a jump on the college application process.[14]

For the most part, the FAFSA utilizes the information on the parents' federal income tax return to assess a student's eligibility for financial aid. It takes into account the student's and parents' income and assets, household size, and the number of family members attending college.[15]

Once the FAFSA has been processed, the student receives an Expected Family Contribution (EFC), which essentially means the amount that parents are expected to be able to pay towards their child's college education. A low EFC score, or dollar amount, means parents can afford to pay very little. A high score, or a relatively high dollar amount, means the parents have an above-average income, and the student will probably not qualify for most Federal financial aid programs.

Financial aid experts consider middle income to be between $40,000 and $65,000.[16] If your family's income exceeds $70,000, your FAFSA or EDC score probably will not be beneficial to you during the scholarship application process. College and university financial aid offices, in particular, rely heavily on the EDC to determine which students receive grants, scholarships and work study.

If your family income increases significantly from one year to the next, your EDC score will increase, which will most likely lead to a decrease in funding for federal educational grant programs. Conversely, if your family income *decreases* substantially from one year to the next, your EDC score will *decrease*, resulting in an *increase* in funding.

If your family has an above-average income, all is not lost. Not all scholarships are based on financial need. For those funded by entities other than the Federal government, such as corporations and non-profit organizations, many are, instead, based on other factors, such as academic performance, demonstrated leadership ability, exemplary community service, a winning essay, an impressive resume, a witty idea, or social media prowess.

For the dozens of scholarship applications we submitted, only about 20 percent requested a copy of the FAFSA or EDC report. Another handful of scholarships had their own financial forms to be completed. The remainder requested no financial information at all, but some requested an explanation of why the student deserved to receive the scholarship as part of an essay.

CHAPTER 7

CREATE THE ALL-IMPORTANT ESSAY

The quality of the scholarship essay is one of the greatest determining factors for the majority of scholarship evaluations. Regardless of the subject matter included in the essay, it should be well written and grammatically correct. But it should also be succinct, unique, and compelling.

The scholarship process would be much easier for students if one essay would suffice for all scholarship applications. Unfortunately, that is not the case. Your basic essay, which will be your personal statement, can be utilized for a large number of scholarship applications. But even the personal statement will need to be tweaked and adjusted to suit the specific requirements of each sponsoring organization.

The selection committee will be looking for originality, creativity, proper spelling, punctuation, and grammar in your essay. It should be positive, hopeful and forward-looking. Also, pay close attention to the specific details about the essay, such as minimum or maximum word count, number of pages, line spacing, and font size.

Elements of the Personal Statement Essay

The personal statement essay will range between 200 to 500 words, depending on the scholarship requirements, and should include the following information:

- Your name, city of origin, name of your h
  or college, and year when you graduated o₁
  graduate

- A summary of your GPA, class rank (if favorable),
  extracurricular activities, honors, and awards

- Leadership activities and positions while in high
  school or college. If you have started a worthwhile
  school or community organization, provide details
  about why and how you established it.

- Information about your intended major or field of
  study, how you became interested in the field, and
  your career goals

- Information about your family background and how it
  has affected your educational goals and attainment

- Your personal interests and hobbies, special skills,
  and talents

- Your involvement in community service projects, the
  nature of the projects, and the number of hours
  expended

- How you expect to use your major after graduation

- Your long-term career goals – Where do you see
  yourself career-wise in five years? Ten years?

- The reason why you wanted to attend college and
  why you deserve to receive the scholarship

- The effect that receiving the award will have on your current and future career plans

Your personal statement essay should always be typewritten, repeatedly massaged and reviewed until it is *perfect*. Elicit the assistance of your English teacher or a family member with strong English skills to assist you in the process. If one of the student's parents possesses strong English skills, this is a tremendous plus. Read the essay aloud to make sure it is interesting and flows smoothly. Revised it as your life's circumstances change and new information, such as extracurricular activities or honors, becomes relevant. The importance of the personal statement essay cannot be over-emphasized.

Expect a Variety of Essay Topics

Many scholarship sponsoring organizations have moved beyond the personal statement essay and have become creative about developing their own specific essay topics. Some are based on the industry in which the entity is positioned; others are based on the student's familiarity with current events or economic trends. Some essays require research on a specific topic, or that they be prepared according to a particular format (e.g., Modern Language Association [MLA] format). Some organizations even seem to be attempting to get student applicants to point them in the direction of the next major market trend, to avoid paying a marketing consultant to do it for them.

During your scholarship quest, you will encounter essay topics that seem to reoccur. For essay topics that you encounter repeatedly, retain the narrative you create for future use. That way, you will not be required to reinvent the wheel each time.

Following are examples of some of the requested essay topics we encountered when we researched scholarship applications:

- How does having purpose affect the quality of your life?

- Why should young people get involved in politics?

- If you had the authority to change your school in a positive way, describe the specific changes you would make.

- Given that you already have the necessities for college, if you could only take what fits into a backpack, what would you bring?

- What do you think the status of the Internet will be in five years? What kind of technology will incorporate Internet access?

- Pick a controversial problem on high school or college/university campuses and suggest a solution.

- How can the Web give a company a competitive advantage?

- Every generation faces new challenges and new problems. What do you think is the biggest difference between your generation and older generations?

- How do you define success and what are your plans to be successful?

- What would you do if you were appointed as chair of a non-profit organization and funded $100,000,000?

- Share a story about how language has helped you express your voice.

- Write about a situation where better safety procedures would have prevented an injury.

- How do you use technology to keep your family connected?

- Explain how you go about honoring America's military heroes.

- Name America's most inspirational military leader and why you believe this individual inspires others.

- Explain how your college experience is or will be enabled by remarkable frugality, ingenuity or thrift.

- How do you consider yourself to be more than just a student?

- Define each of the following competencies and their relative importance to you as you navigate through college and prepare to enter a global society: Cross-cultural aptitude, digital literacy, and financial acumen.

- What do I consider a meaningful contribution, by a citizen, to our society? What will I contribute?

- Consider your favorite quotes, books, movies, music, works of art, etc. Have these influenced your life in a meaningful way?

- What does a credit score mean to you and how do you think you will use it in the future?

- How would you address the issue of United States congressional gridlock?

- How has the Internet helped you with your education?

- If you could start one business to benefit mankind, what would it be and why?

As you can see, the potential essay topics run the gamut, so be prepared for just about any topic you can imagine. With careful planning and time management, the essay submission process will be less cumbersome. Do not procrastinate and wait until the last minute to write your essays. Allow at least a week to prepare a rough draft and finalize the essay to be submitted. Then make plans to submit your application, including the essay, at least a week ahead of the deadline.

In many cases, all or part of one essay can be used for multiple scholarship submissions. Sponsoring organizations require that the essay be original, but most do not require that it be exclusive. This means that as long as the essay represents the student's own work, it can be submitted with numerous scholarship applications.

CHAPTER 8

GET SCHOLARSHIP SPONSORS TO
NOTICE YOUR APPLICATION

Due to the competitive nature of the scholarship process
and the sheer volume of applications that sponsoring
organizations receive, it is imperative that your package
stand out among the rest. Be aware of your strengths and
unique qualities and develop a high-quality presentation that
will catch the selection committee's attention.

During the years that we submitted applications, we
found that scholarships that required applicants to mail in
their packages presented the best opportunity for leveling the
playing field. Mailed-in applications allow the student to
include additional items that could separate him or her from
the pack. The landscape, however, has changed and the vast
majority of scholarship applications are now submitted
online—not via snail mail.

Unless the organization provides a list of requested items
and specifically states, "only include these items and no
others," (or something to that effect), the student is presented
with an opportunity to include additional attention-getting
items. In our case, we had prepared a professional resume
and attached a photography studio head shot. If the
scholarship requested two recommendation letters, we
included four if including more was an option. A copy of an
award certificate for exemplary academic performance or

community service would be another item that would stand out. An original poem written by the student could be an extra item, especially if the scholarship is based upon creativity. If the student received national recognition for exceptional achievements, this information should be highlighted. Be careful not to load too many additional items in the package, but including one or two that can help make the package distinctive can only be a plus.

Some scholarships allow for or even require video submissions as substitutes for or in addition to essay submissions. The video submissions are usually optional, but I believe that, in a competitive environment, a student who submits an essay *and* a high-quality video increases his/her odds of being noticed.

Be sure to read eligibility requirements carefully. There's no point in applying for a scholarship that you are not eligible to receive. If you are uncertain, contact the sponsoring organization.

The more narrow the parameters for the scholarship application, the greater your odds of success. Scholarships that are open to all high school seniors or college students nationwide will have a large pool of applicants and will be extremely competitive. However, scholarships that are more specific, based on a particular major of study, a small segment of the general population (e.g., based on ethnicity), an individual state or a particular college, will have relatively fewer submissions and will not be as competitive.

Some applicants make the mistake of pursuing only the scholarships offering large dollar amounts. Doing so is similar to buying a lottery ticket. Hundreds of thousands of students are chasing the same high-dollar scholarships which provide a full-ride for four years (like the Gates Scholarship), that pay $20,000 total over a six-year period (like the Dell Scholars Program), or that pay $10,000 per year for four years (like the Ron Brown Scholars Program).

As stated previously, it is important to submit as many scholarship applications as possible to as many organizations as possible. The $500 and $1,000 scholarships may seem to be relatively small amounts, but receiving several scholarships at that funding level may provide the cumulative amount you will need to attend college debt-free.

Crowdfunding As An Option

If you are unable to raise the entire amount of college funds needed through the scholarship process, don't despair. The Internet has offered a novel way to raise money, known as crowdfunding. Thousands of individuals have utilized this avenue to finance all sorts of projects, causes, and, yes, college educations.

Put the power of your network of family (both immediate and extended), friends, and social media followers to work and create your own personal scholarship through crowdfunding. By accumulating small donations from lots of people, you may be able to raise the funds required to finance your education.

There are several websites that have been designed specifically for this purpose, including, GoFundMe.com, Indiegogo.com, and Instagrad.

Through **GoFundMe.com**, students can utilize the crowdfunding platform to create a personal donation campaign, share it online, and use the funds raised.[17] The funds can be used for college expenses and even for repaying

student loans. This platform claims to be num[
college tuition fundraising.[18]

There is no fee to set up a campaign; however, GoFundMe.com takes 2.9 percent for processing fees. In addition, there is a fee of $0.30 per transaction.[19]

YouCaring.com has a 120-day limit on the length of fundraisers, but you can run as many as you want. It is possible to get daily access to your funds, so you can apply money toward college expenses or student loans as you go.[20]

✳ **Indiegogo.com** allows students to raise money for whatever they choose. Students can create a campaign, promote it, and watch their money grow.[21]

Be sure to use the funds for the purpose that is advertised. It would be tragic and deceptive for a student to raise money for education through crowdfunding, but not enroll in school, and then use the funds for some other purpose (e.g., to buy a car or go on a vacation). Make your supporters proud of you and glad that they contributed to your success. But keep in mind that your crowdfunding campaign may be unsuccessful.

Internships

Internships provide another avenue to earn funds for college. While some internships offer only course credit and do not provide monetary compensation, many of them include paid stipends, housing and even salaries. Explore your internship options with companies within the industry you are targeting for your career. Internships enhance students' resumes and give them a leg-up when competing for full-time employment upon graduation. More detailed information about internships is included in Chapter 11.

CHAPTER 9

SUBMIT SEPTEMBER - FEBRUARY
SCHOLARSHIP APPLICATIONS

No book that provides guidance regarding the scholarship application process would be complete without a comprehensive listing of scholarship sources. In keeping with this book's title, more than 101 scholarship opportunities are listed in Chapters 9 and 10.

The scholarships listed here can all be applied for directly by the student. They do not require students to go through their high school's guidance counselor or college financial aid office. The links provided go directly to the scholarship page on the organization's web site, whenever possible. Inclusion of these direct links will substantially reduce the amount of time required to search for the specific scholarship and its supporting information. Requirements for each scholarship are listed as bulleted items for easy scanning.

Excluded from this listing are the following categories of scholarships:

- Those based on athletics or participation in team sports;
- Those that require membership in a particular organization or a corporate fee-based membership program;
- Those based upon sweepstakes and random drawings;
- Those based on team projects or competitions; and

- Those that require travel to a particular locale to participate in an oratorical or competitive process in order to receive the award.

The scholarships included in this guide are based on the student's desire for higher education, academic performance, financial need, community service participation, leadership skills, creativity, and/or witty ideas.

Finally, scholarship deadlines are based on the specific dates designated for the 2019-2020 academic year. **It is possible that some of the dates may shift slightly, so checking the sponsoring organization's web site for confirmation of the deadline date is highly recommended.**

YEAR-ROUND OR RECURRING

Central Intelligence Agency (CIA) Undergraduate Scholarship Program
Deadline: Applications accepted year-round

Award Amount: Up to $18,000 per calendar year

No. of scholarships: Varies

Website:
https://www.cia.gov/careers/student-opportunities/undergraduate-scholarship-program.html

Requirements:

- U.S. citizen
- 18 years of age or older by April 1 of senior year in high school
- High school senior planning to enroll in a four- or five-year degree program; or college freshman or

sophomore enrolled in a four- or five-year degree program
- Minimum SAT of 1500, ACT of 21
- Minimum 3.0 GPA
- Demonstrate financial need with household income below $70,000 for a family of four
- Available to work in Washington, DC area during summer
- After college graduation, agree to continue employment with CIA for a period equal to 1.5 times the length of college sponsorship

College Peas Student Standout Scholarship

Deadline: Periodic/Recurring

Award Amount: $400

No. of scholarships: 1

Website: http://www.collegepeas.com/money

Requirements:

- Current high school student who intends to enroll full-time at a four-year college
- Minimum 2.0 GPA

Women's Independence Scholarship Program

Deadline: Accepts applications year-round

Award Amount: Varies

No. of scholarships: Varies

Website: http://wisp.fluidreview.com/

Requirements:

- U.S. citizen or permanent legal resident
- Applied to or officially accepted at an accredited U.S. college or university
- Survived intimate partner abuse and has been separated from their abuser a minimum of one year, but not more than seven
- Demonstrates financial need
- Has a definite plan to use the desired training to upgrade skills for career advancement

SEPTEMBER

Jack & Jill of America Foundation
Deadline: September 6

Award Amount: $1,500 to $2,500

No. of scholarships: Varies

Website: http://www.uncf.org

Requirements:

- African American
- High school senior
- Accepted to or enrolled at accredited four-year college/university

Jones T-Shirts Scholarship
Deadline: September 10

Award Amount: $1,000

No. of scholarships: 1

Website: http://www.jonestshirts.com/scholarship

Requirements: Current student enrolled at a U.S. college or university

The Gates Scholarship

Deadline: September 18

Award Amount: Full college tuition for all four years

No. of scholarships: 300

Website: https://www.thegatesscholarship.org/scholarship

Requirements:

- High school senior
- Ethnic minority (black, Hispanic or Asian)
- U.S. citizen, national, or permanent resident
- Plan to enroll full-time in a four-year degree program at a U.S. accredited, not-for-profit, private or public college or university
- Minimum 3.3 GPA
- Meet Federal Pell Grant eligibility criteria

Ark Law Group Fresh Start Scholarship Program

Deadline: September 21

Award Amount: $1,000

No. of scholarships: 1

Website: http://www.arklawgroup.com/scholarships

Requirement: Enrolled in a two-year, four-year, graduate level or certification program

Catherine W. Pierce/UNCF Scholarship

Deadline: September 28

Award Amount: Up to $4,500

No. of scholarships: Varies

Website: http://www.uncf.org

Requirements:

- U.S. citizen, national, or permanent resident
- Enrolled full-time at a U.S. accredited four-year college or university
- Minimum 2.5 GPA
- Majoring in art or art history

Wm. Wrigley Foundation/UNCF Scholarship

Deadline: September 28

Award Amount: Up to $5,000

No. of scholarships: Varies

Website: http://www.uncf.org

Requirements:

- U.S. citizen, national, or permanent resident
- Attending a UNCF-affiliated university
- College junior, senior, or 5th year senior
- Minimum 2.5 GPA
- Majoring in engineering, business, finance, accounting, chemistry, economics, computer science or marketing

Don't Text and Drive Scholarship

Deadline: September 30

Award Amount: $500 to $1,500

No. of scholarships: 2

Website:
http://www.digitalresponsibility.org/scholarships/

Requirements:

- U.S. citizen or legal resident
- High school student, undergraduate or graduate college student

Key Thinkers Scholarship

Deadline: September 30

Award Amount: $2,500

No. of scholarships: 1

Website: https://www.moneykey.com/scholarship/

Requirements:

- U.S. citizen or permanent resident
- 18 years or older
- Enrolled as a full-time student at an accredited college, university, or trade school in the U.S.
- Minimum 3.0 GPA

OppU Achievers Scholarship

Deadline: September 30

Award Amount: $2,500

No. of scholarships: 1

Website: https://www.opploans.com/scholarship/

Requirements:

- U. S. citizen
- Enrolled full-time in high school or at least part-time in college, graduate, professional, or trade school
- Minimum 3.0 GPA

Writers' Square, Hakka Foundation Essay Contest
Deadline: September 30

Award Amount: $100 to $1,000

No. of scholarships: 15

Website: http://www.writerssquare.org/rules-en

Requirements:

- Division 1: Grades 1-6 (any student enrolled in school)
- Division 2: Grades 7-12 (any student enrolled in school)
- Division 3: College (any student enrolled in college)

OCTOBER

(The) Cash Store Continuing Education Scholarship
Deadline: October 1

Award Amount: $1,000

No. of scholarships: 5

Website: https://www.cashstore.com/scholarship

Requirements:

- Age 25 or older
- High school graduate
- Reside in U.S., Washington, D.C., Puerto Rico or the U.S. Virgin Islands
- Enrolled in full-time undergraduate or graduate study
- Attending accredited two- or four-year college, university or vocational school
- Minimum 2.75 GPA

Knowmad Digital Marketing Scholarship

Deadline: October 1

Award Amount: $500

No. of scholarships: 1

Website: https://www.internationalscholarships.com/3166/Knowmad-Digital-Marketing-Scholarship

Requirements:

- Attend an accredited U.S.-based accredited university
- Undergraduate or graduate student
- Be enrolled in a business, marketing, or communication related degree program

Tom Joyner Foundation Fine Arts Scholarship

Deadline: October 1

Award Amount: $1,000 to $2,000

No. of scholarships: 3

Website:
http://tomjoynerfoundation.org/category/scholarships/

Requirements:

- Attending an HBCU
- Enrolled full-time and in good academic standing

AES Engineering Scholarship

Deadline: October 6

Award Amount: $500

No. of scholarships: 1

Website:
http://www.aesengineers.com/scholarships.htm

Requirements: High school senior, undergraduate or graduate student

Apple HBCU Scholars Program

Deadline: October 7

Award Amount: $25,000 for senior year of study

No. of scholarships: 30

Website:
http://tmcf.org/our-scholarships/current-scholarships/apple-hbcu-scholars-program

Requirements:

- Currently in the second-to-last year of study (juniors or seniors pursuing a fifth year of study)

- Enrolled full-time at a four-year accredited HBCU/PBI
- Minimum 3.3 GPA
- Business, communications, computer science, information science/technology, mathematics, public relations and/or engineering major
- Prior internship experience strongly preferred
- Prior leadership experience

General Mills Graduate Scholarship and Internship

Deadline: October 9

Award Amount: $5,000, plus one paid summer internship with subsidized housing with General Mills

No. of scholarships: 2

Website:
http://www.ift.org/community/students/intern/general-mills-graduate-scholarship-and-internship.aspx

Requirements:

- U.S. citizen or have right to work visa for U.S.
- Full-time graduate student enrolled in M.S. or Ph.D. food science program with an interest in Research and Development and/or Quality
- Minimum 3.0 GPA
- Member of the IFT Student Association at the time of application
- Able to work an 11-12 week internship during summer

GreenPal Business Scholarship

Deadline: October 15

Award Amount: $2,000

No of scholarships: 1

Website:
https://www.yourgreenpal.com/scholarship

Requirements:

- High school senior or college student currently enrolled
- Minimum 3.0 GPA
- Majoring in business
- Started a business while in high school or college

JRC Insurance Group Scholarship

Deadline: October 15

Award Amount: $1,000

No. of scholarships: 1

Website:
http://www.jrcinsurancegroup.com/scholarship/

Requirements:

- At least 17 years of age
- High school senior, or undergraduate student at an accredited, U.S. college/university

Pelican Water Sustainability Scholarship

Deadline: October 15

Award Amount: $500 to $1,500

No. of scholarships: 3

Website:
https://www.pelicanwater.com/scholarship.php

Requirements:

- Legal U.S. resident
- Undergraduate or graduate student
- Currently enrolled full-time at an accredited university in the U.S.

Scholarship America Dream Award

Deadline: October 15

Award Amount: $5,000 to $15,000

No. of scholarships: Varies

Website:
https://scholarshipamerica.org/dreamaward/

Requirements:

- Age 17 or older
- U. S. citizen, permanent resident or deferred action status under DACA
- Undergraduate student at sophomore level or above
- Enrolled in an accredited two- or four-year college, university or vocational-technical school in the U.S.
- Studying to obtain an associate's or first bachelor's degree
- Minimum 3.0 GPA
- Demonstrate financial need

Zavodnick, Zavodnick & Lasky, LLC Future Leaders Scholarship

Deadline: October 15

Award Amount: $1,000

No. of scholarships: 1

Website:
https://www.zavodnicklaw.com/scholarship/

Requirements:

- Legal resident of the United States
- At least 18 years old
- Enrolled in a college, university, or graduate program in the United States at the time of scholarship award

Dr. Pepper Tuition Giveaway

Deadline: October 17

Award Amount: $5,000

No. of scholarships: Varies

Website:
http://www.drpeppertuition.com/program-details

Requirements: Student between the ages of 18-24

Microsoft Research Graduate Women's Scholarship

Deadline: October 17

Award Amount: $18,000, plus a $2,000 conference and travel allowance to attend a conference in their field of study

No. of scholarships: Varies

Website:
https://www.microsoft.com/en-us/research/academic-program/womens-fellowship-program/

Requirements:

- Enrolled in first year as a full-time graduate student in Computer Science, Electrical Engineering, Mathematics, or Bioinformatics/Information Science department
- Must be nominated by their universities, and their nominations must be confirmed by the office of the chair of the department

CVS Health/NMF Pharm.D. Scholarship

Deadline: October 18

Award Amount: $2,500

No. of scholarships: 1

Website: https://nmf.fluidreview.com/

Requirements:

- African-American student
- U.S. citizen or DACA-approved
- Enrolled at an accredited college of pharmacy
- Pursuing a doctorate degree in pharmacy
- Demonstrated financial need

Omega Psi Phi Fraternity International High School Essay Contest

Deadline: October 19

Award Amount: $1,000 to $5,000

No. of scholarships: 4

Website: http://www.oppf.org/essay-contest.asp

Requirements: College-bound high school senior

Michael Jackson/UNCF Scholarship

Deadline: October 21

Award Amount: Up to $5,000

No. of scholarships: Varies

Website: http://www.uncf.org

Requirements:

- U.S. citizen, national, or permanent resident
- Undergraduate or graduate college student
- Attending a UNCF-affiliated university (see website for list)
- Minimum 2.5 GPA
- Majoring in communication arts or social sciences

American Bullion Scholarship Program

Deadline: October 31

Award Amount: $1,000

No. of scholarships: 3

Website:
https://www.americanbullion.com/scholarship/

Requirements:

- U.S. citizen or legal resident
- Undergraduate student
- Enrolled at an accredited U.S. college or university

Bay Alarm Medical Scholarship
Deadline: October 31

Award Amount: $1,000 to $3,500

No. of scholarships: 3

Website:
http://www.bayalarmmedical.com/scholarship

Requirements:

- High school senior or currently enrolled undergraduate student
- Must be involved in a community service effort/volunteer opportunity where you work with the elderly OR
- Must participate in caregiving duties for an elderly relative living in your home

Coca-Cola Scholars Program
Deadline: October 31

Award Amount: $20,000

No. of scholarships: 250

Website:

http://www.coca-colascholarsfoundation.org/applicants/#programs

Requirements:

- U.S. citizen, national, permanent/temporary resident, refugee, asylee, Cuban-Haitian entrant, or humanitarian parolee
- High school senior (home-schooled student may also apply)
- Minimum 3.0 GPA

Liaison's Data-Inspired Future Scholarships

Deadline: October 31

Award Amount: $5,000

No. of scholarships: 1

Website: https://www.liaison.com/scholarship/

Requirements:

- U.S. or Canadian citizen or legal permanent resident
- High school senior or college student (undergraduate or graduate school)
- Enrolled at a U.S. or Canadian college, university or technical school

MyProjectorLamps Scholarship

Deadline: October 31

Award Amount: $500

No. of scholarships: 1

Website:
http://www.myprojectorlamps.com/scholarships.html

Requirements:

- Minimum age of 16 years or older
- High school senior or undergraduate student in U.S.
- Currently attending an accredited U.S. high school or college/university
- Minimum 3.0 GPA
- Must follow or "Like" the MyProjectorLamps Facebook page

NOVEMBER

HubShout Internet Marketing Scholarship

Deadline: November 1

Award Amount: $1,000

No. of scholarships: 1

Website: http://hubshout.com/?p=Scholarship

Requirements:

- College sophomore, junior or senior
- Minimum 3.0 GPA
- Passion for Internet Marketing

Tutor the People Pre-Med Essay Scholarship

Deadline: November 1

Award Amount: $1,000

No. of scholarships: 1

Website: http://tutorthepeople.com/scholarship/

Requirements:

- Attending an educational institution in the U.S.
- Current pre-med undergraduate or future medical school attendee
- Minimum 3.0 GPA

Prudential Spirit of Community Awards

Deadline: November 3

Award Amount: $1,000, plus an all-expense-paid trip with a parent to Washington, D.C. in May 2015

No. of scholarships: 102

Website: http://spirit.prudential.com/view/page/soc/301

Requirements: Students in grades 5-12 who live in the 50 states or Washington, D.C., and have conducted a volunteer service activity within the past year

Foot Locker Foundation Scholarship

Deadline: November 5

Award Amount: $5,000

No. of scholarships: Varies

Website: http://www.uncf.org

Requirements:

- Undergraduate college/university student
- Restricted to United Negro College Fund (UNCF) member institutions
- Minimum 2.5 GPA

Ossie Davis Scholars Program

Deadline: November 9

Award Amount: Up to $6,800

No. of scholarships: Varies

Website: www.uncf.org

Requirements:

- African-American
- U. S. citizen, U.S. national, or permanent resident
- College freshman
- Enrolled at select four-year HBCUs
- Minimum 3.0 GPA
- Majoring in African-American studies, communications, education, fine arts, humanities, performing arts, political science, social sciences, theater arts/drama, visual arts
- Demonstrated financial need

Toyota Financial Services Making Life Easier Scholarship

Deadline: November 13

Award Amount: Up to $20,000

No. of scholarships: 100+

Website:
https://www.scholarsapply.org/toyotafinancial/information.php

Requirements:

- Be between the ages of 16 and 26 as of the application deadline AND be a member, alumnus or staff of one of Toyota's non-profit partners listed on the following web site: https://www.scholarshipamerica.org/toyotafinancial/information.php
- High school senior, graduate, current postsecondary undergraduate, or graduate student
- Have a high school diploma, GED or equivalent
- Plan to enroll in full-time undergraduate or graduate study at an accredited U.S. college or university
- Minimum 2.0 GPA

National Security Agency/Stokes Educational Scholarship Program

Deadline: November 15

Award Amount: Up to $30,000 per year for tuition/fees and a year-round salary

No. of scholarships: Varies

Website:
https://www.intelligencecareers.gov/icstudents.html

Requirements:

- U.S. citizen
- High school senior at the time of application
- Minimum 3.0 GPA
- Minimum SAT of 1600 or ACT of 25

- Majoring in computer science or computer/electrical engineering
- Eligible to be granted a security clearance
- Upon college graduation, must work in your area of study for NSA for at least one-and-one-half times the length of study

Denny's Hungry for Education Scholarship

Deadline: November 16

Award Amount: $1,000

No. of scholarships: Varies

Website: http://www.hacu.net/hacu/scholarships.asp

Requirements:

- Hispanic heritage student
- Full- or part-time undergraduate or graduate student
- Enrolled at two- or four-year HACU-member institution
- Minimum 2.5 GPA
- Reside in one of the following states: AZ, CA, CO, DC., FL, GA, IL, NC, NM, NV, NY, SC, TX, or WA

Jack Kent Cooke Foundation Scholarship

Deadline: November 20

Award Amount: Up to $40,000/year for 4 years

No. of scholarships: 40

Website:
http://www.jkcf.org/scholarship-programs/college-scholarship/

Requirements:

- High school senior
- Planning to enroll at an accredited four-year college or university for the upcoming fall
- Minimum 3.5 GPA
- Minimum SAT combined critical reading and math score of 1200+ and/or ACT composite score of 26+
- Demonstrate financial need

Jack and Jill-Jacqueline Moore Bowles/UNCF Scholarship
Deadline: November 26

Award Amount: $2,250

No. of scholarships: Varies

Website: http://www.uncf.org

Requirements:

- U.S. citizen, national or permanent resident
- African-American student
- Undergraduate junior or senior
- Enrolled full-time at an accredited, post secondary institution
- Minimum 3.0 GPA
- Majoring in communications

Daniels Scholarship Program
Deadline: November 29

Award Amount: Four-year renewable annually; last-dollar scholarship that covers students costs for tuition and fees after other

scholarships, grants, and work study
have been accepted.

No. of scholarships: Varies

Website: https://www.danielsfund.org/scholarships

Requirements:

- U.S. citizen or permanent resident
- High school senior
- Residents of and graduating from a high school in Colorado, New Mexico, Utah and Wyoming only
- Minimum SAT Math score of 470 and Writing score of 450, or a minimum ACT score of 17 in each category
- Demonstrate financial need

American Society of Women Accountants Scholarship (Seattle Chapter)
Deadline: November 30

Award Amount: $2,000 to $4,000

No. of scholarships: 5

Website: http://seattleafwa.org/scholarships/

Requirements:

- Part-time or full-time student pursuing either an associate's, bachelor's or master's degree in accounting
- Attending an accredited community college, college, university or professional school of accounting in the state of Washington
- Completed a minimum of 30 semester hours
- Minimum GPA of 2.05 overall and 3.0 in accounting

Bachus & Schanker, LLC Scholarship

Deadline: November 30

Award Amount: $2,000

No. of scholarships: 1

Website: http://www.coloradolaw.net/scholarship/

Requirements:

- High school senior or undergraduate student
- Accepted to or attending a four-year university
- Minimum 3.0 GPA

Cooper Industries

Deadline: November 30

Award Amount: Varies

No. of scholarships: Varies

Website: http://www.uncf.org

Requirements:

- U.S. citizen, national or permanent resident
- Current undergraduate college student
- Attending an accredited four-year college or university in the U.S.
- Majoring in business or engineering
- Minimum 2.75 GPA

Dede's Do-Over Scholarship

Deadline: November 30

Award Amount: $1,500

No. of scholarships: 10

Website:
https://www.dedemcguirefoundation.org/programs

Requirements:

- Female student
- Age 24 or older
- Low-income or in financial need
- Attending an accredited vocational school, college or university

Education Matters Scholarship
Deadline: November 30

Award Amount: $5,000

No. of scholarships: 1

Website:
https://www.unigo.com/scholarships/our-scholarships/education-matters-scholarship

Requirements:

- Legal resident of the U.S. or the District of Columbia
- Age 13 or older
- Currently enrolled in an accredited post-secondary institution of higher education

DECEMBER

Dell Scholars Program
Deadline: December 1

Award Amount: $20,000 over the course of six years

No. of scholarships: 300

Website: http://www.dellscholars.org

Requirements:

- Participating in a Michael & Susan Dell Foundation approved readiness program in grades 11 and 12 (e.g., IDEA Academy, GEAR UP, Kipp Academy and Upward Bound)
- High school senior graduating from an accredited high school
- Planning to enroll full-time in a bachelor's degree program at an accredited college/university
- Minimum 2.4 GPA
- Demonstrate need for financial assistance
- Eligible to receive federal student aid

ExpoMarketing's Women in Business Scholarship
Deadline: December 1

Award Amount: $1,000

No. of scholarships: 1

Website:
https://www.expomarketing.com/scholarship/

Requirements:

- Female student
- Current undergraduate pursuing a career in business

Herrman & Herrman Innovation Scholarship

Deadline: December 1

Award Amount: $1,000 to $2,500

No. of scholarships: 3

Website:
https://www.herrmanandherrman.com/scholarship/

Requirements:

- High school junior or senior, or undergraduate student
- Undergraduate students must be enrolled at a two- to four-year college or university in the U.S.

Lamber-Goodnow Injury Law Team Education Scholarships

Deadline: December 1

Award Amount: $1,000

No. of scholarships: 8

Website: https://lambergoodnow.com/scholarships/

Requirements:

- Enrolled at an accredited high school, college or university, including four-year, community colleges and junior colleges
- Minimum 2.8 GPA

Minority Scholarship Award for Physical Therapy Students

Deadline: December 1

Award Amount: $5,000

No. of scholarships: 3

Website:
http://www.apta.org/HonorsandAwards/Scholarships/MinorityScholarship/

Requirements:

- Minority student
- College senior or final academic year
- Enrolled in an accredited college or university physical therapist education program

Staver Law Group National Scholarship

Deadline: December 1

Award Amount: $5,000

No. of scholarships: 1

Website:
https://www.chicagolawyer.com/college-scholarship-essay-online-application/

Requirements:

- U.S. citizen
- Enrolled or planning to enroll in a U.S. college or university, or a graduate program within the U.S.
- Minimum 3.0 GPA

Store Coach's Entrepreneur Scholarship

Deadline: December 1

Award Amount: $1,000

No. of scholarships: 1

Website:
https://storecoach.com/coachs-ecommerce-entrepreneur-scholarship

Requirements:

- Full- or part-time college student currently enrolled for the upcoming semester
- Interested in online businesses

Stephen J. Brady Stop Hunger Scholarship

Deadline: December 5

Award Amount: $5,000

No. of scholarships: Varies

Website:
http://www.sodexofoundation.org/hunger_us/scholarships/scholarships.asp

Requirements:

- U.S. citizen or permanent resident
- Student age 5 to 25 (kindergarten through graduate school)
- Enrolled in an accredited U.S. educational institution
- Demonstrate on-going commitment to community by performing unpaid volunteer services impacting hunger in the United States within the last 12 months

Generation Google Scholarship

Deadline: December 6

Award Amount: $10,000

No. of scholarships: Varies

Website:
https://www.google.com/edu/scholarships/the-generation-google-scholarship/

Requirements:

- Ethnic minority (black, Hispanic, American Indian) OR female
- High school senior or currently enrolled as an undergraduate or graduate student
- Plan to be enrolled as a full-time student at a university in the U.S. in the upcoming academic year
- Pursuing a computer science or computer engineering degree, or a degree in a closely related technical field
- Exemplify leadership and a passion for technology
- Exhibit a strong record of academic achievement

Center for Alcohol Policy Essay Contest

Deadline: December 7

Award Amount: $1,000 to $5,000

No. of scholarships: 3

Website:
http://www.centerforalcoholpolicy.org/essay-contest/

Requirements: Contest is open to all persons who are over the age of 18 as of November 2018. Students, academics, practicing attorneys, policymakers, and members of the general public are encouraged to submit essays.

Ship Smart Scholarship

Deadline: December 7

Award Amount: $300 to $1,000

No. of scholarships: 4

Website:
https://www.shipsmart.com/info/scholarship

Requirements:

- Current full-time or part-time students
- Enrolled at an accredited, non-accredited institute, truck driving school, or other logistics program
- Minimum 3.0 GPA

Google Lime Scholarship

Deadline: December 8

Award Amount: $5,000 to $10,000

No. of scholarships: 16

Website: http://www.limeconnect.com

Requirements:

- Student with visible or invisible disability
- Current full-time undergraduate, graduate or PhD student enrolled at a university in the U.S. or Canada
- Pursuing a computer science or computer engineering degree, or a degree in a closely related technical field
- Strong academic performance
- Demonstrated leadership and commitment and passion for computer science and technology

PWC Lime Scholarship

Deadline: December 9

Award Amount: $4,000

No. of scholarships: Varies

Website: http://www.limeconnect.com

Requirements:

- Student with visible or invisible disability
- Current full-time undergraduate (freshman, sophomore, or junior) student enrolled at a four-year university in the U.S.
- Pursuing a degree in accounting, computer, engineering, math, finance, or economics
- Minimum 3.0 GPA
- Demonstrated leadership and commitment and passion for accounting, computer science and/or technology

Mobility Scooters Direct Scholarship Program

Deadline: December 10

Award Amount: $1,500

No. of scholarships: 1

Website:
https://www.mobilityscootersdirect.com/scholarship

Requirements:

- At least 18 years of age
- Currently enrolled in a minimum of 6 hours undergraduate or 3 hours graduate at an accredited college or university
- Minimum 3.0 GPA
- Have proof of a declared major
- Demonstrate involvement on campus or in the community of attended institution

iWP Clean Water Scholarship

Deadline: December 12

Award Amount: $1,000

No. of scholarships: 1

Website: https://iwaterpurification.com/scholarship/

Requirements:

- Attending an accredited university in the United States, Canada, Australia or the United Kingdom
- Enrolled in or previously acquired a credit in any course related to environmental science, biology, engineering, film and art, law, international politics, or chemistry

- Minimum 2.5 GPA
- Demonstrate financial need

Artificial Grass Liquidators Scholarship

Deadline: December 15

Award Amount: $1,000

No. of scholarships: 1

Website:
http://www.artificialgrassliquidators.com/scholarship/

Requirement: Currently enrolled in an accredited
college

AXA Achievement Scholarship (In Association with *U.S. News & World Report*)

Deadline: December 14

Award Amount: $10,000

No. of scholarships: 52

Website:
https://www.scholarshipamerica.org/axa-achievement/information.php

Requirements:

- U.S. citizen or legal resident
- High school senior planning to enroll in an accredited two- or four-year college/university in the U.S. for the entire upcoming academic year
- Demonstrate ambition and self-drive as evidenced by outstanding achievement in school, community or work-related activities

Burger King Scholars

Deadline:	December 15
Award Amount:	$12,500 per academic year for up to four years
No. of scholarships:	2,000
Website:	http://www.bkmclamorefoundation.org

Requirements:

- Resident of U.S., Canada or Puerto Rico
- Graduating high school senior only
- Planned enrollment in accredited two- or four-year college in fall
- Minimum 2.5 GPA

Creative Safety Supply Scholarship

Deadline:	December 15
Award Amount:	$1,000
No. of scholarships:	1

Website:
https://www.creativesafetysupply.com/scholarship/

Requirements:

- U.S. citizen or permanent resident
- Enrolled in a college, university, or vocational school for the upcoming term
- Minimum 3.0 GPA

Foreclosure.com Scholarship

Deadline: December 15

Award Amount: First place - $2,500; Second and Third
                         Place - $500 each

No. of scholarships: 3

Website: http://www.foreclosure.com/scholarship

Requirements: Currently enrolled undergraduate
                         college students (graduate students,
                         law students and/or high school
                         seniors are *not* eligible)

QuikshipToner.com Student Scholarship

Deadline: December 15

Award Amount: $1,500

No. of scholarships: 1

Website:
http://www.quikshiptoner.com/catalog/scholarship_program.php

Requirements:

- U.S. citizen
- Student enrolled in an undergraduate or graduate
  degree program at any accredited U.S. college,
  university or trade school

Sachs Marketing Group General Marketing Education Scholarship

Deadline: December 15

Award Amount: $1,000

No. of scholarships: 1

Website:
https://sachsmarketinggroup.com/general-marketing-education-scholarship-marketing-education/

Requirement: Any student currently enrolled in any accredited college

Westwind Recovery Scholarship
Deadline: December 15

Award Amount: $1,000

No. of scholarships: 1

Website:
https://www.westwindrecovery.com/about-westwind/general-education-scholarship

Requirement: Currently enrolled in an accredited college

(The) Christophers College Video Contest
Deadline: December 17

Award Amount: $100 to $2,000

No. of scholarships: 8

Website:
http://www.christophers.org/page.aspx?pid=273

Requirements: Enrolled in and attending undergraduate or graduate college classes, full or part time, between Sept. 1 and Dec. 15

SingleCare Medical Scholarship

Deadline: December 21

Award Amount: $1,000

No. of scholarships: 3

Website: https://www.singlecare.com/scholarship

Requirements:

- Currently enrolled or planning to enroll in a medical program in the upcoming semester
- Attending an accredited medical school program, pharmacy school program, or nursing school program in the U.S.

National World War II Museum Essay Contest

Deadline: December 28

Award Amount: $500 to $1,000

No. of scholarships: 3

Website:
http://www.nationalww2museum.org/learn/education/for-students/essay-contests/

Requirement: High school students in the U.S., U.S. territories, and military bases

EK Insurance Scholarship

Deadline: December 30

Award Amount: $500

No. of scholarships: 1

Website: https://ekinsurance.com/scholarship/

Requirements:

- U. S. citizen or permanent legal resident
- Enrolled full-time and in good academic standing at an accredited two-year or four-year college or university or in an accredited graduate school program

Fitwirr College Scholarship

Deadline: December 30

Award Amount: $1,000

No. of scholarships: 1

Website:
https://www.fitwirr.com/lifestyle/college-scholarship/

Requirements:

- U.S. resident
- Currently enrolled in a U.S. accredited college or university

Kitchen Cabinet Kings Entrepreneur Scholarship

Deadline: December 30

Award Amount: $5,000

No. of scholarships: 1

Website:
https://kitchencabinetkings.com/scholarship

Requirements:

- Current college student or incoming freshman enrolled in an undergraduate or graduate degree program
- Attending an accredited American college, university or grade school

Vape Craft Inc. Scholarship

Deadline: December 30

Award Amount: $4,000

No. of scholarships: 1

Website: https://vapecraftinc.com/scholarships

Requirements:

- Age 18 or older
- Currently enrolled at a college or university
- In good standing, demonstrating academic excellence
- Minimum 2.8 GPA

Achieve Today Scholarship Fund

Deadline: December 31

Award Amount: $1,000

No. of scholarships: 1

Website:
http://www.achievetoday.com/scholarships

Requirements: Current student at an accredited U.S. college or university

Active Life Scholarship for Financial Literacy

Deadline: December 31

Award Amount: $1,000

No. of scholarships: 1

Website:
http://www.getupgetactive.org/scholarship/

Requirements: Current college, graduate school or adult learners

AfterCollege Business Student Scholarship

Deadline: December 31

Award Amount: $500

No. of scholarships: Varies

Website:
http://www.aftercollege.com/content/scholarships

Requirements:

- Currently enrolled college/university student
- Minimum 3.0 GPA
- Majoring in business fields, including accounting, advertising, business administration, economics, finance, human resources, international relations, management, political science, public relations, etc.

AfterCollege STEM Inclusion Scholarship

Deadline: December 31

Award Amount: $1,000

No. of scholarships: Varies

Website:
http://www.aftercollege.com/content/scholarships

Requirements:

- Currently enrolled college/university student
- Minimum 3.0 GPA
- Majoring in science fields, including technology, engineering, mathematics

Caring.com Student-Caregiver Scholarship
Deadline: December 31

Award Amount: $1,500

No. of scholarships: 2

Website:
https://www.caring.com/senior-living/assisted-living#scholarship

Requirements:

- Enrolled at an accredited U.S. college or university
- Caring for an adult relative or an aging loved one

CC Bank's Young Scholars Scholarship
Deadline: December 31

Award Amount: $2,000

No. of scholarships: 5

Website: https://ccbank.us/scholarship/

Requirements:

- U.S. resident
- Under the age of 30
- Minimum 3.0 GPA
- Enrolled in an academic institution

Direct Energy Live Brighter Scholarship

Deadline: December 31

Award Amount: $2,500 to $5,000

No. of scholarships: 3

Website: https://www.directenergy.com/scholarship

Requirements:

- Registered college student for the upcoming academic year
- 18 years of age or older
- Resident of one of the following states: CT, DE, IL, IN, MD, MA, MI, NJ, NY, OH, PA, TX, NH, RI and DC
- Minimum 3.0

Emroch & Kilduff, LLP Scholarship

Deadline: December 31

Award Amount: $1,000

No. of scholarships: 1

Website: https://emrochandkilduff.com/scholarship/

Requirements: High school senior planning to enroll in an accredited U.S. college or university during the upcoming academic year

Gen and Kelly Tanabe Scholarship

Deadline: December 31

Award Amount: $1,000

No. of scholarships: 3

Website: http://www.genkellyscholarship.com

Requirements:

- U.S. citizen or legal resident
- High school student from 9th to 12th grade OR undergraduate or graduate college student

HeadsetPlus.com Annual College Scholarship

Deadline: December 31

Award Amount: $1,000

No. of scholarships: 1

Website: http://headsetplus.com/newsdesk95/newsdesk_info.html

Requirements:

- U.S. citizen
- Age 16 or older
- High school senior entering college, current college students or graduate students
- Minimum 3.0 GPA

iVein Health & Wellness Scholarship

Deadline: December 31

Award Amount: $2,500

No. of scholarships: 1

Website: https://www.ivein.com/scholarship/

Requirements:

- Current full-time undergraduate/graduate student
- Attending an accredited U.S. university or college
- Minimum 3.4 GPA

Key Thinkers Scholarship
Deadline: December 31

Award Amount: $2,500

No. of scholarships: 1

Website: https://www.moneykey.com/scholarship/

Requirements:

- U.S. citizen or permanent resident
- 18 years or older
- Enrolled as a full-time student at an accredited college, university, or trade school in the U.S.
- Minimum 3.0 GPA

Maple Holistics Natural Scholarship
Deadline: December 31

Award Amount: $1,000

No. of scholarships: 1

Website:
https://www.mapleholistics.com/scholarship/

Requirements: Student enrolled in a high school, college, university or trade school

Mattress Fun Yearly Scholarship
Deadline: December 31

Award Amount: $1,000

No. of scholarships: 1

Website:
http://www.handsonmattress.com/best-mattress-yearly-scholarship/

Requirements:

- Current high school (or home-schooled) senior attending school in the United States OR current college student already studying at an accredited U.S. post-secondary institution
- Minimum 3.0 GPA

M.S. Woods Scholarship
Deadline: December 31

Award Amount: $1,500

No. of scholarships: 1

Website:
https://www.mswoods.com/scholarship.htm

Requirements: Student attending or accepted to an official, accredited U.S. college or university

OppU Achievers Scholarship

Deadline: December 31

Award Amount: $2,500

No. of scholarships: 1

Website: https://www.opploans.com/scholarship/

Requirements:

- U. S. citizen
- Enrolled full-time in high school or at least part-time in college, graduate, professional, or trade school
- Minimum 3.0 GPA

Promises Treatment Centers Scholarship

Deadline: December 31

Award Amount: $1,000 to $6,000

No. of scholarships: 3

Website:
https://www.promises.com/scholarship/#apply

Requirements:

- Legal U.S. resident
- At least 18 years old
- Currently enrolled or have been accepted to enroll as an undergraduate in a college or university in the U.S.

Tobi Cares Scholarship

Deadline: December 31

Award Amount: $3,000

No. of scholarships: 1

Website:
http://www.tobi.com/#scholarship_program

Requirements:

- Female students only
- Enrolled or enrolling as an undergraduate student at a four-year college or community college in the U.S.
- Incoming freshman, sophomore, junior or senior

JANUARY

Decaso Furniture Company Future Quest Scholarship

Deadline: January 1

Award Amount: $2,500

No. of scholarships: 1

Website:
https://www.decaso.com/pages/scholarship-application-future-quest

Requirements:

- High school senior, college undergraduate, or graduate student
- Enrolled or planning to enroll at an accredited two-year, four-year, or technical/vocational college or university in the U.S.
- Minimum 2.0 GPA

Fundera College Scholarship for Student Entrepreneurs

Deadline: January 1

Award Amount: $2,000

No. of scholarships: 1

Website:
https://www.fundera.com/resources/fundera-scholarship

Requirements:

- Current or incoming college student
- Enrolled at a university in the U.S. and able to provide documentation to confirm enrollment

Joseph J. LoRusso College Scholarship

Deadline: January 1

Award Amount: $1,000

No. of scholarships: 1

Website: https://injuryflorida.lawyer/scholarship/

Requirements:

- High school senior or current college student
- Attending an accredited U.S. college or university in fall of upcoming academic year

Jones T-Shirts Scholarship

Deadline: January 7

Award Amount: $1,000

No. of scholarships: 1

Website: http://www.jonestshirts.com/scholarship

Requirements: Current student enrolled at a U.S. college or university

Switzer Environmental Fellowship
Deadline: January 7

Award Amount: $15,000

No. of scholarships: Varies

Website:
https://www.switzernetwork.org/become-fellow

Requirements:

- U.S. citizen
- Full-time graduate student enrolled in environmental-related course study
- Attending an accredited graduate institute in one of the following states: CA, CT, MA, ME, NH, RI or VT
- Very strong academic qualifications

Ron Brown Scholar Program
Deadline: January 9

Award Amount: $40,000 ($10,000 each year for four years)

No. of scholarships: 10 to 20

Website: http://www.ronbrown.org

Requirements:

- African American
- U.S. citizen or permanent resident
- Current high school senior
- Demonstrate financial need
- Demonstrate academic achievement
- Exhibit leadership ability
- Participate in community service activities

Asian & Pacific Islander American Scholarship Fund

Deadline: January 10

Award Amount: $2,500 to $20,000

No. of scholarships: Varies

Website:
http://www.apiasf.org/scholarship_apiasf.html

Requirements:

- Asian and/or Pacific Islander ethnicity as defined by the U.S. Census
- U.S. citizen or legal resident
- Enrolling as an undergraduate student in a U.S. accredited college or university in the fall of the upcoming academic year
- Minimum 2.7 GPA

American Association for Paralegal Education (AAfPE) Scholarship

Deadline: January 14

Award Amount: $500

No. of scholarships: 5

Website:
http://www.aafpe.org/?page=LEXScholarship

Requirements:

- Full-time or part-time student attending a school that has a LEX (Lambda Epsilon Chi) Honor Society Chapter
- Pursuing a paralegal education

John Lennon Endowed Scholarship
Deadline: January 14

Award Amount: Up to $5,000

No. of scholarships: Varies

Website: www.uncf.org

Requirements:

- U.S. citizen, national or permanent resident
- Current undergraduate student
- Enrolled at a UNCF-member institution
- Majoring in communications, mass communications, mass media arts, music or performing arts
- Minimum 3.0 GPA

Distillery Scholarship Program
Deadline: January 15

Award Amount: $1,000

No. of scholarships: 1

Website: https://distillery.com/scholarship-program

Requirements:

- Undergraduate or graduate student
- Attending an accredited four-year university
- Declared major in computer science, computer engineering, software engineering, IT or a related field of study

Feldco Windows, Siding and Doors Scholarship

Deadline: January 15

Award Amount: $1,000

No. of scholarships: 1

Website: http://www.4feldco.com/scholarship/

Requirements:

- Legal U.S. resident
- Current undergraduate college student or a current high school student that will be enrolled in college in the coming academic year

Providian Medical Scholarship

Deadline: January 15

Award Amount: $500

No. of scholarships: 2

Website:
http://www.providianmedical.com/providian-medical-scholarship/

Requirements:

- U.S. citizen
- Age 16 or older
- Current high school senior or undergraduate student
- Attending or planning to attend a U.S. college or university
- Minimum 3.0 GPA

Washington Crossing Foundation Scholarship
Deadline: January 15

Award Amount: $500 to $5,000

No. of scholarships: Varies

Website:
http://www.gwcf.org/SchlProgram.html

Requirements:

- U.S. citizen
- High school senior
- Planning career in local, state or federal government service

Greg Goff Leadership Awards (NSHSS Foundation)
Deadline: January 16

Award Amount: $1,000

No. of scholarships: Varies

Website:
http://nshssfoundation.org/scholarships/greg-goff-leadership-awards/

Requirements:

- High school senior
- Minimum 3.0 GPA
- Open to students worldwide

John F. Kennedy Profile in Courage Scholarship

Deadline: January 18

Award Amount: First Place - $10,000
Second Place - $1,000
Third Place - $500 (five finalists)

No. of scholarships: 7

Website:
http://www.jfklibrary.org/Education/Profile-in-Courage-Essay-Contest.aspx

Requirements:

- U.S. citizen
- High school student grade nine through twelve attending public, private, parochial, or home schools; OR
- Under the age of twenty enrolled in a high school correspondence/GED program in any of the 50 states, the District of Columbia, or the U.S. territories; or attending school overseas

Girls Impact the World Film Festival Scholarship

Deadline: January 20

Award Amount: $1,000 to $5,000

No. of scholarships: Varies

Website:
http://www.connecther.org/gitw/guidelines

Requirements:

- Females only
- Full-time high school student or enrolled undergraduate student
- Maximum age of 25 as of Dec. 31
- International students from all countries, including the U.S., with the exception of the following: Cuba, Iran, North Korea, Sudan and Syria

Tom Joyner Foundation Full-Ride Scholarship
Deadline: January 20

Award Amount: All expenses for four years

No. of scholarships: 1

Website:
http://tomjoynerfoundation.org/category/scholarships/tjf-full-ride-scholars/

Requirements:

- U.S. citizen
- High school senior
- Accepted at Historically Black College or University (HBCU) by July 1
- Minimum 3.5 GPA
- Minimum SAT score of 2100 or ACT score of 30

UNCF/Malcolm X Scholarship for "Exceptional Courage"
Deadline: January 28

Award Amount: Up to $4,000

No. of scholarships: Varies

Website: http://www.uncf.org

Requirements:

- U.S. citizen, national or permanent resident
- College freshman, sophomore, junior, senior, or 5th year senior
- Enrolled at a UNCF-affiliated institution
- Minimum 2.5 GPA

Technology Addiction Awareness Scholarship
Deadline: January 30

Award Amount: $500 to $1,500

No. of scholarships: 2

Website:
http://www.digitalresponsibility.org/scholarships/

Requirements:

- U.S. citizen or legal resident
- High school student, undergraduate or graduate college student

ACIS Travel Is Education Scholarship
Deadline: January 31

Award Amount: $500 to $1,000

No. of scholarships: 4

Website: http://www.acis.com/students/scholarships

Requirements:

- Student in grades 6 through 12
- Have traveled on an ACIS tour in the past year

Chegg's New Year's Resolution Scholarship
Deadline: January 31

Award Amount: $1,000

No. of scholarships: 1

Website:
http://www.chegg.com/scholarships/cheggs-1000-new-years-resolution-scholarship

Requirements: Current U.S. high school senior

CoffeeForLess.com "Hit the Books" Scholarship
Deadline: January 31

Award Amount: $500

No. of scholarships: 1

Website:
http://www.coffeeforless.com/scholarship

Requirements:

- Age 18 to 25
- Enrolled in accredited college/university

I Have a Dream Scholarship
Deadline: January 31

Award Amount: $1,500

No. of scholarships: 1

Website:
https://www.unigo.com/scholarships/our-scholarships/i-have-a-dream-scholarship

Requirements:

- Age 13 or older
- Legal U.S. resident
- Currently enrolled in an accredited post-secondary institution of higher education, or enrolled no later than the fall of 2023

Payscale Scholarship

Deadline: January 31

Award Amount: $2,000

No. of scholarships: 1

Website:
http://www.payscale.com/education/scholarship

Requirements:

- Female applicants only
- Enrolled in an associate, bachelor's or graduate level program
- Majoring in S.T.E.M. related disciplines

Redfin Scholarship

Deadline: January 31

Award Amount: $2,500

No. of scholarships: 1

Website:
https://www.redfin.com/resources/scholarship

Requirements:

- Legal U.S. resident
- Graduating high school senior or current freshman, sophomore, or junior in college attending an accredited university or college
- Minimum 3.5 GPA

Return2College Scholarship
Deadline: January 31

Award Amount: $1,000

No. of scholarships: 1

Website:
http://www.return2college.com/awardprogram.cfm

Requirements:

- U.S. citizen or legal resident
- Age 17 or older; no maximum age limit
- Plan to enroll or be enrolled full or part time at a college or university within 12 months after scholarship award

UNCF/UBS-Paine Webber Scholarship
Deadline: January 31

Award Amount: Up to $8,000

No. of scholarships: Varies

Website: http://www.uncf.org

Requirements:

- U.S. citizen, national, or permanent resident
- College sophomore or junior
- Enrolled at a UNCF-affiliated institution
- Minimum 3.0 GPA
- Majoring in accounting, business, business-related, economics, finance, international business, management or marketing

FEBRUARY

Epsilon Sigma Alpha Foundation
Deadline: February 1

Award Amount: $550 to $7,500

No. of scholarships: Varies

Website:
http://www.epsilonsigmaalpha.org/scholarships-and-grants/scholarships

Requirements:

- Minimum 3.0 GPA OR a minimum SAT of 1030 or ACT of 22
- The Foundation has a number of various endowments with their own separate criteria

Intel Scholarship
Deadline: February 1

Award Amount: Up to $5,000

No. of scholarships: Varies

Website: www.uncf.org

Requirements:

- African-American
- U. S. citizen
- College sophomore, junior or senior, master's student
- Enrolled at four-year accredited college or university
- Minimum 3.2 GPA
- Majoring in computer engineering, computer information systems, computer science, electrical engineering, information technology or mechanical engineering
- Demonstrated financial need (Pell Grant eligible)

JRC Insurance Group Scholarship
Deadline: February 1

Award Amount: $1,000

No. of scholarships: 1

Website:
http://www.jrcinsurancegroup.com/scholarship/

Requirements:

- At least 17 years of age
- High school senior, or undergraduate student at an accredited, U.S. college/university

Zeta Phi Beta National Educational Foundation

Deadline: February 1

Award Amount: $500 to $1,000

No. of scholarships: Varies

Website:
http://www.zpbnef1975.org/scholarships--descriptions.html

Requirements: Graduating high school senior or
                         undergraduate college student
                         attending school full-time

NOTE: Zeta chapters in most cities also offer local
scholarships. Contact the chapter in your city for further
details.

Center for Advancing Opportunity Undergraduate Research Scholarship

Deadline: February 3

Award Amount: Up to $7,500

No. of scholarships: Varies

Website: http://www.tmcf.org

Requirements:

- U.S. citizen or permanent resident
- Enrolled full-time at any four-year HBCU
- Rising college junior or senior as of previous fall
  semester
- Majoring in business, criminal justice, economics,
  education, philosophy, political science, or sociology
- Minimum 3.5 GPA

Jimmy Rane Foundation

Deadline: February 6

Award Amount: $500 to $5,000

No. of scholarships: Varies

Website:
https://www.jimmyranefoundation.org/scholarship

Requirements:

- U.S. citizen or permanent resident
- No older than 20 as of August 1
- Graduating high school senior or college student at accredited college/university
- 3.0 GPA for graduating high school senior/2.75 GPA for college student
- Resident of one of the following states: AL, AR, DC, DE, FL, GA, IA, KS, KY, LA, MD, MO, MS, NC, NE, NJ, NY, OH, OK, PA, SC, TN, TX, VA, WV
- Student athletes are *not* eligible

RMEL Foundation Scholarship

Deadline: February 7

Award Amount: $3,000

No. of scholarships: Varies

Website:
https://www.rmelfoundation.org/scholarships/

Requirements:

- U.S. citizen or permanent resident
- High school senior, high school graduate, or college undergraduate
- Be pursuing or plan to pursue an undergraduate degree with intent to pursue a career in the electric energy industry

Finnegan Diversity Scholarship for Law Students

Deadline: February 8

Award Amount: $15,000

No. of scholarships: 1

Website: http://www.finnegan.com/diversity/

Requirements:

- Minority student based on either race, ethnicity, disability or sexual orientation
- Enrolled in an ABA-accredited law school
- Undergraduate degree in life sciences/chemistry, engineering, or computer science

AHLEF Hospitality Graduate School Scholarship

Deadline: February 14

Award Amount: $5,000

No. of scholarships: 16

Website:
https://www.ahlef.org/scholarships/academic-scholarships

Requirements:

- U.S. citizen or permanent resident
- Possess a hospitality-related undergraduate degree or four years' employment in the lodging industry after graduation
- Enrolled full- or part-time in a U.S. college or university
- Minimum 3.0 GPA

Alzheimer's Foundation for America Teens for Alzheimer's Awareness College Scholarship

Deadline: February 15

Award Amount: $500 to $5,000

No. of scholarships: 10

Website: https://alzfdn.org/young-leaders-of-afa/afa-teens/scholarship-contest/

Requirements:

- U.S. citizen or permanent resident
- High school senior
- Must enter a four-year accredited college or university within 12 months of the application deadline

Hyatt Hotels Fund for Minority Lodging Management Students

Deadline: February 15

Award Amount: $500 to $7,500

No. of scholarships: Varies

Website:
https://www.ahlef.org/academic-scholarships

Requirements:

- Minority student (African-American, Hispanic, Native American, or Asian/Pacific Islander)
- Pursuing a bachelor's degree in hospitality management
- At least a junior in a four-year undergraduate program for the upcoming fall semester

The Jackie Robinson Foundation Scholarship
Deadline: February 15

Award Amount: $7,500 per year for up to four years

No. of scholarships: Varies

Website: http://www.jackierobinson.org

Requirements:

- High school senior
- Enrollment at accredited four-year college/university

The Levin Law Firm Scholarship
Deadline: February 15

Award Amount: $1,000

No. of scholarships: 1

Website:
http://www.levininjuryfirm.com/scholarship/

Requirement: Currently attending or planning to attend an accredited college, university or graduate school in the U.S.

Society of Women Engineers Scholarship Program

Deadline: February 15 (college soph and above)
May 1 (entering college freshmen)

Award Amount: $1,000 to $10,000

No. of scholarships: Varies

Website:
http://societyofwomenengineers.swe.org/scholarships

Requirements:

- Women only
- Planning to study an ABET-accredited program in engineering, technology, or computing in the upcoming academic year
- Planning to attend full time (exceptions are made for reentry and non-traditional applicants)
- Not fully funded for tuition, fees, and books and equivalent

George and Mary Josephine Hamman Foundation Scholarship

Deadline: February 16

Award Amount: $16,000 disbursed over four years

No. of scholarships: 70

Website:
http://hammanfoundation.org/scholarship-guidelines/

Requirements:

- Houston-area high school senior
- U.S. citizen
- Demonstrate academic ability and financial need

Simon Youth Community Scholarship

Deadline: February 20

Award Amount: $1,500

No. of scholarships: 50+

Website: http://programs.applyists.com/syf/

Requirements:

- High school senior attending school and living within 50 miles of the Simon or Washington Prime property associated with the application
- Legal U.S. resident
- Plan to enroll full-time in an accredited two- or four-year college, university or vocational/technical school in the coming academic year
- Demonstrate academic promise and financial need

Dr. Wynetta A. Frazier "Sister to Sister" Scholarship

Deadline: February 28

Award Amount: $1,000

No. of scholarships: 1

Website: http://www.nhbwinc.com/scholarship.html

Requirements:

- African-American female
- Age 25+
- Returning to college after education was interrupted by family responsibilities or other personal demands

Dr. Edward Jacobson Healthy Living Scholarship
Deadline: February 28

Award Amount: $500

No. of scholarships: 1

Website:
https://www.greenwichgynecology.com/dr-edward-jacobson-healthy-living-scholarship/

Requirements:

- High school graduate, undergraduate or graduate student
- Enrolled at an accredited community college, junior college, undergraduate, or graduate institution in the United States
- Minimum 3.0 GPA
- Able to articulate ways student embodies the principles of healthy living

LaGrant Foundation Undergraduate Scholarship
Deadline: February 28

Award Amount: $2,500

No. of scholarships: Varies

Gwen Richardson

Website:
http://www.lagrantfoundation.org/Undergraduate%20Scholarships

Requirements:

- Ethnic minority (African American, Asian American, Pacific Islander, Hispanic/Latino, Native American/Alaska Native)
- U.S. citizen or permanent resident
- Undergraduate college freshman, sophomore, junior or non-graduating senior
- Full-time student at four-year, accredited institution within the U.S., carrying a total of 12 units or more per semester/quarter
- Minimum 3.0 GPA
- Majoring in one of the following fields: Public relations, marketing or advertising, anthropology, communications, English, graphic design, or sociology
- If chosen, applicant MUST attend TLF's scholarship three-day summer activities to receive scholarship.

Optimist International Essay Contest

Deadline: February 28

Award Amount: Varies

No. of scholarships: Varies

Website:
http://www.optimist.org/e/member/scholarships3.cfm

Requirements: High school student under age of 18

Youth Foundation, Inc./Hadden Scholarship

Deadline: February 28

Award Amount: $2,500 to $4,000

No. of scholarships: Varies

Website: http://fdnweb.org/youthfdn/

Requirements:

- Graduating U.S. high school senior
- Enrolled at accredited four-year college/university
- Minimum 3.5 GPA
- Demonstrate financial need

CHAPTER 10

SUBMIT MARCH – AUGUST
SCHOLARSHIP APPLICATIONS

MARCH

American Chemical Society Scholars Program
Deadline: March 1

Award Amount: Up to $5,000

No. of scholarships: 100

Website:
http://www.acs.org/content/acs/en/funding-and-awards/scholarships/acsscholars.html

Requirements:

- African American, Hispanic or Native American
- U.S. citizen or permanent resident
- High school senior and college student
- Attending an accredited college/university on a full-time basis
- Minimum 3.0 GPA
- Majoring in chemistry, biochemistry, chemical engineering, materials science, environmental science or toxicology
- Demonstrate financial need

Dr. Blanca Moore-Velez Woman of Substance Scholarship

Deadline: March 1

Award Amount: $1,000

No. of scholarships: 1

Website:
http://www.nanbpwc.org/index-11.html

Requirements:

- African American female
- Age 35+
- U.S. citizen
- Undergraduate student enrolled in an accredited college or university
- Minimum 3.0 GPA

Dr. Julianne Malveaux Scholarship

Deadline: March 1

Award Amount: $1,000

No. of scholarships: 1

Website:
http://www.nanbpwc.org/index-11.html

Requirements:

- African American female
- U.S. citizen
- College sophomore or junior enrolled in an accredited college or university
- Minimum 3.0 GPA
- Majoring in journalism, economics or related field

Gallery Collection Annual Create-A-Greeting-Card Scholarship Contest

Deadline: March 1

Award Amount: $10,000, plus $1,000 for school

No. of scholarships: 1

Website:
http://www.gallerycollection.com/greeting-cards-scholarship.htm

Requirements:

- U.S. citizen or legal resident
- Age 14 or older
- High school, college or university student

HubShout Internet Marketing Scholarship

Deadline: March 1

Award Amount: $1,000

No. of scholarships: 1

Website: http://hubshout.com/?p=Scholarship

Requirements:

- College sophomore, junior or senior
- Minimum 3.0 GPA
- Passion for Internet Marketing

Jeannette Rankin Women's Scholarship Fund

Deadline: March 1

Award Amount: $2,000

No. of scholarships: 80+

Website:
https://rankinfoundation.org/for-students

Requirements:

- U.S. citizen or permanent resident
- Female, age 35 or older
- Pursuing a technical or vocational education, an associate's degree, or a first bachelor's degree
- Enrolled in, or accepted to, a regionally or ACICS accredited school
- Low-income

National Association of Negro Business and Professional Women's Clubs, Inc. (NANBPWC) National Scholarship

Deadline: March 1

Award Amount: Varies

No. of scholarships: Varies

Website:
http://www.nanbpwc.org/index-11.html

Requirements:

- African American
- U.S. citizen
- High school senior
- Minimum 3.0 GPA

National Press Club Scholarship For Journalism Diversity

Deadline: March 1

Award Amount: $2,000

No. of scholarships: 3

Website:
http://press.org/about/scholarships/diversity

Requirements:

- High school senior
- Minimum 3.0 GPA
- Majoring in journalism

Print and Graphics Scholarship Foundation

Deadline: March 1

Award Amount: $2,000 to $5,000

No. of scholarships: 200

Website: https://pgsf.org/

Requirements:

- High school senior or graduate, or undergraduate college student
- Enrolled in a two- or four-year accredited graphic or printing program at a technical school, college or university within the U.S., attending full time
- Pursuing a career in graphic communications, printing technology, printing management or publishing

Society of Exploration Geophysicists (SEG) Foundation Scholarship

Deadline: March 1

Award Amount: Ranges from $500 to $14,000 per academic year

No. of scholarships: Varies

Website: http://seg.org/Scholarships

Requirements:

- High school senior; undergraduate or graduate college student
- Above average grades (merit-based)
- Planning to pursue a college curriculum directed toward a career in applied geophysics or a closely related field, such as geosciences, physics, geology, or earth and environmental sciences

UNCF STEM Scholars Program

Deadline: March 3

Award Amount: $2,500 to $5,000

No. of scholarships: 100

Website: www.uncf.org

Requirements:

- African American
- High school senior
- U.S. citizen or permanent legal resident
- Majoring in engineering, mathematics, science or technology

- Minimum 3.0 GPA in math and science courses
- Demonstrated financial need

Nebraska Broadcasters Association Foundation Student Scholarship

Deadline: March 4

Award Amount: $2,000

No. of scholarships: 2

Website:
https://www.ne-ba.org/default-nbaf_studentscholarshipprogram.asp

Requirements:

- Must have a Nebraska connection—either graduated from a Nebraska high school or attending a Nebraska college or university
- Attending a four-year public or private college or university
- Majoring in broadcasting, communications, or a related field
- Planning a career in radio or television broadcasting

Irene S. Wischer Educational Foundation Scholarship

Deadline: March 7

Award Amount: Up to $10,800 per year

No. of scholarships: Varies

Website:
https://www.frostbank.com/Pages/wischer-scholarship.aspx

Requirements:

- U.S. citizen
- Legal resident of Texas for 12 consecutive months prior to application submission
- Demonstrate good character; preference will be given to "applicants who are Christians and attend church regularly"
- Demonstrate academic ability
- Demonstrate financial need

Carroylin and Robert Threlkel Scholarship

Deadline: March 8

Award Amount: $1,000 to $5,000

No. of scholarships: Varies

Website:
https://sacregcf.academicworks.com/opportunities/637

Requirements:

- Female student
- Currently enrolled full-time in an accredited college, university or community college
- Pursuing a business-related undergraduate degree
- Minimum 2.5 GPA
- Demonstrate financial need

Eugene and Thora Chin Scholarship

Deadline: March 8

Award Amount: $1,000 to $5,000

No. of scholarships: Varies

Website:
https://sacregcf.academicworks.com/opportunities/641

Requirements:

- Asian/Pacific Islander heritage
- Plan to attend an accredited two- or four-year college, university, or graduate school
- Minimum 4.0 GPA in high school or 3.5 GPA in college
- Demonstrated financial need

(The) Graydon and Myrth Fox Scholarship

Deadline: March 8

Award Amount: $1,000 to $5,000

No. of scholarships: Varies

Website:
https://sacregcf.academicworks.com/opportunities/631

Requirements:

- Veteran who has served honorably in the U.S. Armed Forces, a surviving spouse, dependent child or grandchild of a U.S. veteran
- Deceased or wounded personnel must have been performing official military duties in a combat situation or a military training exercise
- Pursuing a degree at an accredited college, university or trade school
- Demonstrate financial need

American Association of Blacks in Energy Scholarship

Deadline: March 15

Award Amount: $5,000

No. of scholarships: Varies

Website:
http://aabe.org/index.php?component=pages&id=4

Requirements:

- Minority student
- High school senior
- Entering an accredited college/university
- Minimum 3.0 GPA
- Majoring in business, technology, engineering, mathematics, or one of the physical sciences

Andeavor Youth Leadership Awards (NSHSS Foundation)

Deadline: March 15

Award Amount: $2,500

No. of scholarships: 20

Website:
http://nshssfoundation.org/scholarships/andeavor-youth-leadership-awards/

Requirements:

- U.S. citizen or permanent resident
- Graduating high school senior
- Minimum 3.0 GPA
- Demonstrated financial need

- Permanent resident of one of the following 19 states where Tesoro does business: AK, AZ, CA, CO, ID, IA, MN, MT, NE, NV, NM, ND, OR, SD, TX, UT, WA, WI, WY

Association For Women In Science (Seattle) Scholarship

Deadline: March 15

Award Amount: $1,000 to $5,000

No. of scholarships: 4 to 7 per year

Website: http://seattleawis.org/award/scholarships/

Requirements:

- Applicants must have a U.S.-issued social security number
- College junior or senior at a four-year college or university
- State of Washington institution
- Declared major in the sciences, engineering or mathematics
- Demonstrated financial need

Dunkin' Donuts Scholarship Program

Deadline: March 15 (later in some locales)

Award Amount: Varies

No. of scholarships: Varies

Website:
http://www.dunkindonuts.com/content/dunkindonuts/en/scholarship.html

Requirements:

- High school senior
- Positive academic record, demonstrated leadership, commitment to school and community activities
- Residents of Rhode Island, Connecticut, and Massachusetts (by March 15); residents of New Hampshire and Greater Philadelphia (by April 15); Greater Miami, Ft Lauderdale and Ft Myers (by April 29).

HomeAdvisor Skilled Labor Shortage Scholarship
Deadline: March 15

Award Amount: $2,500

No. of scholarships: 6

Website:
https://www.homeadvisor.com/r/scholarships/#.WSNDd1Pyto6

Requirements:

- High school senior who has been accepted to a college or trade school
- Student currently enrolled in an undergraduate or graduate degree program at an accredited college, university, or trade school in the United States

National Restaurant Association Educational Foundation Scholarship
Deadline: March 15

Award Amount: $2,500

No. of scholarships: Varies

Website:
https://chooserestaurants.org/Programs-and-Scholarships/Undergraduate-Scholarships

Requirements:

- U.S. citizen or permanent resident
- Full-time undergraduate college student
- Enrolled or accepted at an accredited post-secondary institution, college, or university
- Majoring in restaurant or hospitality industry-related field
- Plan to be enrolled for at least two consecutive terms

Stewart J. Guss College Student Scholarship
Deadline: March 15

Award Amount: $1,000

No. of scholarships: 1

Website:
http://attorneyguss.com/annual-stewart-j-guss-college-student-scholarship/

Requirements: Aspiring or current college student

Delta Sigma Theta Research and Educational Foundation/Mentoring Keys Scholarship
Deadline: March 21

Award Amount: $5,000 over a two-year period

No. of scholarships: Varies

Website:
http://www.deltafoundation.net/charitable-engagement-services/scholarships-and-internships

Requirements:

- High school seniors and/or undergraduate students
- Attend Historically Black College or University (HBCU)
- Minimum 3.0 GPA
- Student pursuing a bachelor's degree in business related disciplines
- Multiple scholarships available, some with residency requirements in specific states

NOTE: Delta chapters in most cities also offer local scholarships. Contact the chapter in your city for further details.

Astronaut Scholarship Foundation Program

Deadline: March 25

Award Amount: Up to $10,000

No. of scholarships: 50

Website:
https://astronautscholarship.org/scholarshipprogram.html

Requirements:

- U.S. citizen
- College sophomore or junior
- Enrolled in one of the participating universities (see website for list)

- Seeking a STEM degree with intentions to pursue research or advance field upon completion of final degrees
- Student planning to pursue a practice in professional medicine is *not* eligible

Don't Mess With Texas Scholarship

Deadline: March 26

Award Amount: Grand Prize - $6,000; Two additional $2,000 scholarships

No. of scholarships: 3

Website:
http://www.dontmesswithtexas.org/education-overview/scholarships/

Requirements:

- High school senior
- Current Texas resident
- Planning to pursue a two- or four-year degree at an accredited Texas college or university

CVS Pharmacy, Inc. Business Scholarships

Deadline: March 30

Award Amount: $5,000

No. of scholarships: Varies

Website: http://www.uncf.org

Requirements:

- U.S. citizen, permanent resident or foreign national
- Minimum 3.0 GPA
- Pursuing undergraduate degree in accounting, business, finance, human resources
- Demonstrate unmet financial need

International Association of Black Actuaries Scholarship
Deadline: March 30

Award Amount: $3,000 to $5,000

No. of scholarships: 1

Website: https://www.blackactuaries.org/

Requirements:

- Black student of African descent
- U.S. citizen or permanent resident; Canadian citizen or permanent resident; or citizen of Caribbean or African nation on U.S. or Canadian student visa
- Admitted to a college or university in the U.S. or Canada offering a program in actuarial science or preparation for actuarial career
- Minimum 3.0 GPA
- Minimum math score of 600 on SAT or 28 on ACT
- Attempted or already passed an actuarial exam

Paul S. Mills Scholarship
Deadline: March 30

Award Amount: $1,000

No. of scholarships: 3 to 6

139

Website:
https://www.financialpro.org/foundation/Awards/psm.htm

Requirements:

- U.S. citizen or legal resident
- Full- or part-time student enrolled or accepted into an undergraduate college or university program
- Pursuing course study in a financial service field, such as accounting, finance, insurance or risk management, actuarial sciences, and related fields of business
- Demonstrate financial need by submitting FAFSA or similar documentation

Albert W. Dent Graduate Student Scholarship

Deadline: March 31

Award Amount: $5,000

No. of scholarships: 15

Website:
https://www.ache.org/career-resource-center/special-groups/resources-for-students-and-early-careerists

Requirements:

- U. S. citizen
- Minority student
- Enrolled full-time in a healthcare management graduate program—MHA, MPH, MBA in healthcare administration or similar
- Entering final year of full-time study
- Demonstrate financial need

Aspiring Writers/Go On Girl Book Club Scholarship

Deadline: March 31

Award Amount: $1,000

No. of scholarships: 1

Website:
https://goongirl.org/scholarships/aspiring-writer

Requirements:

- U.S. citizen or resident alien
- Strong connection to identify with the African Diaspora
- Full-time student at an HBCU
- Minimum 2.5 GPA

DREAM Act Scholarship

Deadline: March 31

Award Amount: $500

No. of scholarships: Varies

Website: http://thevisafirm.com/scholarship/

Requirements:

- Enrolled in a community college, private or public undergraduate college or university, graduate program, business school or law school in the U.S.
- Minimum 3.0 GPA

Germans from Russia Heritage Society Essay Contest

Deadline: March 31

Award Amount: $100 to $1,000

No. of scholarships: 6

Website:
http://grhs.org/youthn/current/current.html

Requirements: Open to middle school, high school and college/university undergraduates from around the world.

Key Thinkers Scholarship

Deadline: March 31

Award Amount: $2,500

No. of scholarships: 1

Website: https://www.moneykey.com/scholarship/

Requirements:

- U.S. citizen or permanent resident
- 18 years or older
- Enrolled as a full-time student at an accredited college, university, or trade school in the U.S.
- Minimum 3.0 GPA

OppU Achievers Scholarship

Deadline: March 31

Award Amount: $2,500

No. of scholarships: 1

Website: https://www.opploans.com/scholarship/

Requirements:

- U. S. citizen
- Enrolled full-time in high school or at least part-time in college, graduate, professional, or trade school
- Minimum 3.0 GPA

Writers' Square, Hakka Foundation Essay Contest
Deadline: March 31

Award Amount: $100 to $1,000

No. of scholarships: 15

Website: http://www.writerssquare.org/rules-en

Requirements:

- Division 1: Grades 1-6 (any student enrolled in school)
- Division 2: Grades7-12 (any student enrolled in school)
- Division 3: College (any student enrolled in college)

APRIL

Accounting & Financial Women's Alliance Scholarship
Deadline: April 1

Award Amount: $1,000 to $3,000

No. of scholarships: 8 to 10

Website:
http://www.afwa.org/foundation/scholarships/#.VPJHRyx0zct

Requirements:

- College junior, senior or fifth-year accounting students only. Must have completed sophomore year of study.
- Majoring in accounting or finance
- Minimum 3.0 GPA
- Demonstrate financial need

NOTE: Local AFWA chapters also award scholarships. Check with the chapter in your local area for additional scholarship opportunities.

Champion Energy Scholars Scholarship
Deadline: April 1

Award Amount: $2,000 to $5,000

No. of scholarships: 3

Website:
http://www.championenergyservices.com/programs/scholarship/

Requirements:

- High school senior
- Planning to attend an accredited two- or four-year college degree program
- Minimum 3.0 GPA
- Resident of Texas

The Charles, Lela and Mary Slough Foundation Scholarship
Deadline: April 1

Award Amount: Up to $5,000 per year for a total of 5 years

No. of scholarships: Varies

Website:
https://comptroller.texas.gov/programs/education/msp/fundin g/aid/scholarship/ssloughfoundation.php

Requirements:

- Texas resident only
- Student entering or enrolled in accredited colleges/universities anywhere in the U.S.
- Demonstrate financial need

Davis-Putter Scholarship
Deadline: April 1

Award Amount: $1,000 to $10,000

No of scholarships: 30

Website:
http://www.davisputter.org/apply/apply-for-scholarships/

Requirements:

- High school senior, or college/university student at the undergraduate or graduate level
- Demonstrate financial need
- Must be active in a movement for social and/or economic justice

Herbert Lehman Education Fund Scholarship
Deadline: April 1

Award Amount: $5,000

No. of scholarships: Varies

Website:
http://www.naacpldf.org/herbert-lehman-education-fund-scholarship

Requirements:

- African American
- U.S. citizen
- High school senior, high school graduate, student entering college for first time or beginning their sophomore year in college
- Attending accredited four-year college/university

National Society of Accountants Scholarship Foundation
Deadline: April 1

Award Amount: $500 to $2,200

No. of scholarships: Approximately 30

Website:
http://www.nsacct.org/about/nsa-scholarship-foundation

Requirements:

- U.S. or Canadian citizen
- Undergraduate enrolled part-time or full-time in accounting at an accredited two- or four-year college/university in the U.S.
- Minimum 3.0 GPA
- Majoring in accounting

Project Yellow Light Scholarship (Sponsored by Mazda)
Deadline: April 1

Award Amount: $1,000 to $5,000

No. of scholarships: 6

Website: http://projectyellowlight.com/

Requirements: High school junior or senior, or undergraduate student at two- to four-year accredited college/university or technical school

Thurgood Marshall College Fund and Ford Blue Oval Scholarship

Deadline: April 1

Award Amount: $6,200

No. of scholarships: Varies

Website: http://www.tmcf.org

Requirements:

- African-American male
- High school senior
- Enrolling full-time as a freshman at an HBCU in the coming fall semester
- Minimum 3.0 GPA
- Demonstrate financial need
- Demonstrated leadership ability

Virginia Society of Certified Public Accountants Scholarship

Deadline: April 1

Award Amount: $1,000 to $5,000

No. of scholarships: 15+

Website: https://www.vscpa.com/scholarships

Requirements:

- U.S. citizen
- Enrollment in an accredited Virginia college or university accounting program
- Successful completion of 3 credit hours of accounting prior to application

William E. Wilson Graduate School Scholarship

Deadline: April 1

Award Amount: $5,000

No. of scholarships: 1

Website:
https://www.setc.org/scholarships-awards/graduate-studies/wilson-award/

Requirements:

- Legal resident of one of the following states: AL, FL, GA, KT, MS, NC, SC, TN, VA, or WV
- At least one year of experience as a full-time teacher and director of theatre in a secondary school in one of the above states
- Enrolled in an accredited graduate program within one of the above states within one year of being selected for scholarship

Johnnie T. Melia Memorial Scholarship

Deadline: April 11

Award Amount: $1,000

No. of scholarships: 1

Website:
https://www.jtmeliamoving.com/jt-melia-scholarship-information-a-469.html

Requirement:

- High school or college student that intends to take college courses during the upcoming fall semester

Texas Floral Endowment
Deadline: April 11

Award Amount: $500 to $1,000

No. of scholarships: Varies

Website: http://www.tsfa.org/scholarships.html

Requirements:

- Texas resident only
- High school senior
- Interested in entering the field of horticulture or floriculture

Signet Classics Student Scholarship Essay Contest
Deadline: April 14 (Postmark)

Award Amount: $1,000

No. of scholarships: 5

Website:
http://www.penguin.com/services-academic/essayhome/

Requirements:

- High school junior or senior
- Ages 16 to 18
- Attending high school located in the 50 United States and the District of Columbia OR
- Home-schooled students located in the 50 United States and the District of Columbia

Alpha Kappa Alpha (AKA) Capitalized Endowment Fund Scholarships
Deadline: April 15

Award Amount: Varies

No. of scholarships: Varies

Website:
https://akaeaf.org/scholarships

Requirements:

- Full-time, college sophomore or beyond, including graduate students
- Enrolled at accredited degree-granting institution
- Minimum 3.0 GPA for merit-based scholarships; 2.5 GPA for financial need-based scholarships
- Demonstrate community service and involvement

NOTE: AKA chapters in most cities also offer local scholarships. Contact the chapter in your city for further details.

Children's Cause for Cancer Advocacy Scholarship
Deadline: April 15

Award Amount: $2,000

No. of scholarships: 2

Website: https://www.childrenscause.org/scholars/

Requirements:

- Childhood cancer survivor
- U.S. citizen or legal resident
- Age 25 or under
- Pursuing a bachelor's degree or higher

Kelly & Soto Law Scholarship
Deadline: April 15

Award Amount: $200 to $1,000

No. of scholarships: 3

Website:
http://www.1800lawguys.com/scholarships/

Requirements:

- U.S. citizen residing in the United States, or a legal permanent resident
- Accepted to an institution of higher learning
- High school senior registered at a U.S. high school, or a current college student enrolled at a two- or four-year accredited U.S. institution

LEAD Scholarship Foundation
Deadline: April 15 (deadline varies in April)

Award Amount: $3,500 to $5,000

No. of scholarships: 5 to 7

Website: http://www.leadscholarshipfoundation.com

Requirements:

- U.S. citizen
- African-American student
- High school senior
- Planning to attend an accredited two- or four-year college or university
- Minimum 3.0 GPA
- Provide evidence of scholarly achievement and extensive community service
- Possess strong communication skills
- Demonstrate financial need
- Maintain a minimum 3.0 GPA during first semester of college (scholarship funds are awarded only after submitting first semester transcript)

Masergy STEM Scholarship

Deadline: April 15

Award Amount: $5,000

No. of scholarships: 1

Website:
https://www.masergy.com/stem-scholarship/

Requirements:

- Undergraduate or graduate student currently attending or planning to attend an accredited four-year college or university in the U.S.
- Majoring in a STEM field

MyProjectorLamps Scholarship

Deadline: April 15

Award Amount: $500

No. of scholarships: 1

Website:
http://www.myprojectorlamps.com/scholarships.html

Requirements:

- Minimum age of 16 years or older
- High school senior or undergraduate student in U.S.
- Currently attending an accredited U.S. high school or college/university
- Minimum 3.0 GPA
- Must follow or "Like" the MyProjectorLamps Facebook page

National Society of High School Scholars Foundation

Deadline: April 15

Award Amount: $1,000

No. of scholarships: 25+

Website: http://nshssfoundation.org

Requirements:

- High school senior
- Minimum 3.0 GPA

Pelican Water Sustainability Scholarship

Deadline: April 15

Award Amount: $500 to $1,500

No. of scholarships: 3

Website:
https://www.pelicanwater.com/scholarship.php

Requirements:

- Legal U.S. resident
- Undergraduate or graduate student
- Currently enrolled full-time at an accredited university in the U.S.

The Verbal Ink Transcription Services Scholarship

Deadline: April 15

Award Amount: $1,500 (renewable annually for up to four years)

No. of scholarships: 1

Website:
http://verbalink.com/transcription-services-scholarship

Requirements:

- Graduating high school senior or college freshman
- Enrolled at accredited two- or four-year institution
- Minimum 3.0 GPA

Zavodnick, Zavodnick & Lasky, LLC Future Leaders Scholarship

Deadline: April 15

Award Amount: $1,000

No. of scholarships: 1

Website:
https://www.zavodnicklaw.com/scholarship/

Requirements:

- Legal resident of the United States
- At least 18 years old
- Enrolled in a college, university, or graduate program in the United States at the time of scholarship award

Carl N. & Margaret Karcher (Carl's Jr.)Founders' Scholarship

Deadline: April 16

Award Amount: $10,000

No. of scholarships: 6

Website: http://www.carlsjr.com/scholarship

Requirements:

- High school senior or graduate who plans to enroll **for the first time** in full-time undergraduate study
- Age 21 and under
- Attending an accredited four-year college or university for the entire upcoming academic year
- Resident of Alaska, Arizona, California, Colorado, Hawaii, Idaho, Louisiana, Nevada, New Mexico, New York, Oklahoma, Oregon, Texas, Utah, Washington or Wyoming

Atlas Shrugged Essay Contest

Deadline: April 18

Award Amount: First prize - $2,000; 5 Second Prizes - $500; 10 Third Prizes - $200; 45 Finalists - $50; 175 Semifinalists - $30

No. of scholarships: 236 Total

Website: https://www.aynrand.org/students/essay-contests

Requirements:

- Open to students worldwide
- Eighth, ninth and tenth graders

Attorney Ronald D. Weiss College Scholarship

Deadline: April 21

Award Amount: $2,500

No. of scholarships: 1

Website: https://www.ny-bankruptcy.com/scholarship/

Requirements:

- Currently enrolled in a college or university or planning to enroll as a freshman for the upcoming academic year
- Be in good academic standing with current educational institution
- If under 18, permission from parent or guardian is required

Negative Population Growth Essay Scholarship

Deadline: April 23

Award Amount: $1,000 to $2,500

No. of scholarships: Varies

Website: http://npg.org/scholarships.html

Requirements:

- U.S. citizen
- Age 14 or older
- High school senior, or college freshman, sophomore or junior
- Enrolled in or attending an accredited school within the U.S. or operated overseas by the U.S. government

Ark Law Group Fresh Start Scholarship Program

Deadline: April 30

Award Amount: $1,000

No. of scholarships: 1

Website: http://www.arklawgroup.com/scholarships

Requirement: Enrolled in a two-year, four-year, graduate level or certification program

Brown/MAE Health Care Scholarship

Deadline: April 30

Award Amount: $1,000

No. of scholarships: 1

Website: http://brownmae.org/scholarships/

Requirements:

- Minority student (African-American, Native American, Hispanic, or Asian-Pacific Islander)
- Interested in pursuing a health care career
- Minimum 3.0 GPA

Brown/MAE Teaching Scholarship

Deadline: April 30

Award Amount: $1,000

No. of scholarships: 1

Website: http://brownmae.org/scholarships/

Requirements:

- Minority student (African-American, Native American, Hispanic, or Asian-Pacific Islander)
- Interested in pursuing a teaching career
- Minimum 3.0 GPA

DietsinReview.com Scholarship

Deadline: April 30

Award Amount: $1,000 to $3,500

No. of scholarships: 3

Website:
https://www.dietsinreview.com/scholarship/

Requirements:

- U.S. citizen, U.S. national, U.S. permanent resident, refugee, Cuban-Haitian entrant, or Humanitarian Parolee
- 14 years old or older
- Currently enrolled in a U.S. accredited college, university, or trade school

E-Waste Scholarship

Deadline: April 30

Award Amount: $500 to $1,500

No. of scholarships: 2

Website:
http://www.digitalresponsibility.org/scholarships/

Requirements:

- U.S. citizen or legal resident
- High school student, undergraduate, or graduate college student

International Association of Plumbing and Mechanical Officials (IAPMO) Scholarship

Deadline: April 30

Award Amount: $500 to $1,000

No. of scholarships: 3

Website:
http://www.iapmo.org/Pages/EssayContest.aspx

Requirements: High school senior, or full-time student at accredited technical/trade school, community college, four-year college/university, apprentice program

Joshua David Gardner Memorial Scholarship Endowment

Deadline: April 30

Award Amount: $2,000

No. of scholarships: 2

Website: http://www.joshgardnerendowment.org

Requirements:

- African American
- Between ages of 17 and 25
- High school senior or college student
- Minimum 3.0 GPA
- SAT score of 1,500 or greater
- ACT score of 23 or greater

MillerCoors/TMCF Scholarship

Deadline: April 30

Award Amount: $6,200

No. of scholarships: Varies

Website: http://tmcf.org

Requirements:

- U.S. citizen
- 21 years of age or older
- Full-time student at one of TMCF's 47 member schools (HBCUs)
- Minimum 3.0 GPA
- Demonstrated financial need
- Demonstrated leadership ability

National Black McDonald's Owners Association Hospitality Scholars Program
Deadline: April 30

Award Amount: Up to $5,000

No. of scholarships: Varies

Website: http://www.uncf.org

Requirements:

- African American
- U.S. citizen
- College freshman, sophomore or junior
- Attend Historically Black College or University (HBCU)
- Minimum 2.8 GPA
- Majoring in accounting, business, hospital management, hotel management, marketing or restaurant management

Norman O. Brown Scholarship
Deadline: April 30

Award Amount: $1,000

No. of scholarships: 1

Website: http://brownmae.org/scholarships/

Requirements:

- Minority student (African-American, Native American, Hispanic, or Asian-Pacific Islander)
- Minimum 2.0 GPA
- Demonstrate financial need

Ovid Scholarship
Deadline: April 30

Award Amount: $500 to $1,500

No. of scholarships: 6

Website: https://www.ovidlife.com/scholarship

Requirements:

- Current or incoming undergraduate or graduate student
- Enrolled in an accredited U.S. college, university, or trade/vocational school
- Minimum 3.0 GPA

Shawn Carter Scholarship Foundation
Deadline: April 30

Award Amount: $1,500 to $2,500

No. of scholarships: Varies

Website: http://www.shawncartersf.com

Requirements:

- U.S. citizen or permanent resident
- 25 years old or younger
- High school or college student, student with G.E.D. diploma or at vocational school
- Minimum 2.0 GPA

Sigma Gamma Rho Sorority National Education Fund, Inc.

Deadline: April 30

Award Amount: Varies

No. of scholarships: Varies

Website: https://www.sgrnationaleducationfund.org/scholarships

Requirements:

- High school senior or undergraduate student
- Demonstrate financial need

NOTE: SGR chapters in most cities also offer local scholarships. Contact the chapter in your city for further details.

Snowdrop Foundation

Deadline: April 30

Award Amount: $500 to $5,000

No. of scholarships: 75

Website:
http://snowdropfoundation.org/our-cause/snowdrop-scholarship-program/

Requirements:

- Pediatric cancer patient or survivor diagnosed before the age of 21
- Incoming college undergraduate or graduate student

Soliant's Sunrise Scholarship
Deadline: April 30

Award Amount: $1,000

No. of scholarships: 1

Website:
http://www.soliantconsulting.com/about-soliant/soliants-sunrise-scholarship

Requirements:

- High school senior accepted to an accredited U.S. two-year or four-year college or university OR currently enrolled undergraduate student
- Minimum 3.0 GPA

Western Union Foundation Scholarship
Deadline: April 30

Award Amount: $2,500

No. of scholarships: Varies

Website:
https://foundation.westernunion.com/wuscholars/index.html

Requirements:

- Ages 18 to 26 (on June 1 prior to the academic year)
- Enrolled or admitted to an accredited post-secondary institution seeking an undergraduate degree
- Pursuing a degree/field of study in one of the following: science, technology, engineering, mathematics, or business/entrepreneurship

MAY

1800Wheelchair.com Scholarship

Deadline: May 1

Award Amount: $500

No. of scholarships: 2

Website:
http://www.1800wheelchair.com/scholarship

Requirements:

- Age 16 years or older
- Currently enrolled in good standing as a high school senior or undergraduate student
- Enrolled at an accredited U.S. high school, college or university
- Minimum 3.0 GPA

Cancer Support Scholarship for Cancer Survivors

Deadline: May 1

Award Amount: $5,000

No. of scholarships: 1

Website:
http://www.lepfoundation.org/#!applications/cihc

Requirements:

- U. S. citizen or resident
- Student diagnosed with cancer in childhood (letter of confirmation from physician required)
- Accepted or enrolled in a U.S. college or university

DutchCrafters Amish Furniture Heritage Scholarship
Deadline: May 1

Award Amount: $500

No. of scholarships: 3

Website:
http://www.dutchcrafters.com/heritage-scholarship

Requirements:

- U.S. citizen or legal resident
- High school or college student
- Enrolled in accredited four-year college/university
- Minimum 3.0 GPA
- Demonstrate financial need

Faith, Hope and Love Jesus Inc. Scholarship
Deadline: May 1

Award Amount: $500

No. of scholarships: 1

Website:
http://faithhopeandlovejesus.org/college_scholarship

Requirements:

- Student accepted or enrolled in an undergraduate program at an accredited college or university
- Physician's documentation of history of a blood disorder or cancer diagnosed before the age of 18

John Lepping Memorial Scholarship for Disabled Youth
Deadline: May 1

Award Amount: Up to $5,000

No. of scholarships: 1

Website:
http://www.lepfoundation.org/#!applications/cihc

Requirements:

- Residents of NY, NJ or PA ONLY
- Disabled youth, including but not limited to physical disabilities and psychological handicaps (letter of confirmation from physician required)
- Accepted or enrolled in a U.S. college or university

Monsanto Graduate Student Scholarship
Deadline: May 1

Award Amount: $25,000

No. of scholarships: 1

Website:
https://monsanto.com/careers/student-opportunities/student-scholarships/

Requirements:

- Enrolled or admitted in a Master of Science degree program with emphasis in S.T.E.M.
- Enrolled or admitted to an accredited college or university in the U.S.

Stoddard Firm Legal Scholarship

Deadline: May 1

Award Amount: $2,000

No. of scholarships: 1

Website:
https://thestoddardfirm.com/legal-scholarship/

Requirements:

- First-year law student
- U.S. citizen or authorized to work in the U.S.
- Commencing law school in upcoming fall semester

Vivint Smart Home Scholarship

Deadline: May 1

Award Amount: $1,000

No. of scholarships: 5

Website:
http://www.vivint.com/scholarship

Requirements:

- High school senior or college student
- U.S. citizen or legal resident

- Majoring in one of the following disciplines: Accounting, Architecture, Art, Art History, Business, Engineering, Computer Science, Communications, Creative Writing, Economics, Education, English, Graphic Design, History, Humanities, Information Systems, Public Relations, Journalism, Marketing, Mathematics, Law, Health Care, Political Science, Psychology, Philosophy, Social Work, Film Studies, Digital Media, Language, Theater, Web Design, Women's and Gender Studies

Asia SiVon Cottom Memorial Scholarship Fund
Deadline: May 6

Award Amount: $500 to $2,000 (renewable)

No. of scholarships: Varies

Website: http://asiacottom.com/scholarship-fund/

Requirements:

- U.S. citizen
- High school senior entering an accredited U.S. college/university, OR returning college student attending an accredited U.S. college/university, OR graduate student attending an accredited U.S. college/university
- Minimum 3.0 GPA
- Pursuing a degree with a concentration in STEM

UNCF/KAT Team Foundation Scholarship
Deadline: May 11

Award Amount: $1,000 (renewable for 4 years)

No. of scholarships: 4

Website: http://www.uncf.org

Requirements:

- U.S. citizen, national, or permanent resident
- High school senior
- Accepted at any accredited four-year institution
- Minimum 2.8 GPA
- Demonstrate financial need

TMCF/Honda Scholarship Program
Deadline: May 13

Award Amount: $5,000

No. of scholarships: Varies

Website: http://www.tmcf.org

Requirements:

- U.S. citizen or permanent resident
- Full-time undergraduate student
- Enrolled at an HBCU
- Majoring in engineering, supply chain management, and/or manufacturing

AdmitSee Scholarship
Deadline: May 15

Award Amount: $5,000

No. of scholarships: 1

Website:
https://www.admitsee.com/high-school-college-scholarships

Requirements:

- At least 13 years of age
- Enrolled at a high school or college in the U.S.

Lowe's Scholarship (Thurgood Marshall College Fund)
Deadline: May 15

Award Amount: $500 to $7,500

No. of scholarships: Varies

Website:
https://tmcf.org/our-scholarships/current-scholarships/tmcf-lowes-gap-scholarship/5459

Requirements:

- U.S. citizen or permanent legal resident
- Undergraduate sophomore, junior or senior
- Attending an HBCU
- Demonstrate a combination of financial need and merit
- At risk of not returning to school or graduating due to an outstanding financial need
- Have an outstanding balance remaining on their account

Steven Scher Memorial Scholarship for Aspiring Restauranteurs
Deadline: May 15

Award Amount: $8,000

No. of scholarships: Varies

Website:
https://www.jamesbeard.org/scholarships

Requirements:

- U.S. citizen or resident
- High school senior or graduate
- Planning to enroll or already enrolled full- or part-time during upcoming academic year
- Course of study leading to a certificate or degree at a licensed or accredited culinary school

DiBella Law Offices, P.C. Scholarship
Deadline: May 16

Award Amount: $500

No. of scholarships: 1

Website:
https://www.dibellalawoffice.com/scholarship/application.php

Requirements:

- High school senior or undergraduate student
- U.S. citizen or permanent resident
- Minimum 3.0 GPA

Congressional Black Caucus (CBC) Spouses Scholarship
Deadline: May 19

Award Amount: Varies

No. of scholarships: Varies

Website:
https://cbcfinc.academicworks.com/opportunities/180

Requirements:

- U.S. citizen or permanent resident
- Currently enrolled or planning to enroll as full-time undergraduate or graduate student at accredited college/university
- Minimum 2.5 GPA
- Exhibit leadership ability and participate in community service activities

Thermo Scientific Pierce Scholarship Award
Deadline: May 20

Award Amount: $5,000 to $10,000

No. of scholarships: 6

Website:
http://www.pierce-antibodies.com/PierceScholarship/index.cfm

Requirements:

- Enrolled as an undergraduate or graduate student at an accredited college or university
- Minimum 3.0 GPA
- Majoring in biology, chemistry, biochemistry or a related life science field

Costco Scholarship (Thurgood Marshall College Fund)
Deadline: May 21

Award Amount: $7,200

No. of scholarships: Varies

Website: https://tmcf.org/our-scholarships

Requirements:

- U.S. citizen or legal resident
- Full-time undergraduate student enrolled at one of TMCF's 47 HBCU member schools
- Minimum 3.0 GPA
- Demonstrated leadership qualities and community service experience

Hershey Company Scholarship (Thurgood Marshall College Fund)

Deadline: May 21

Award Amount: $6,200

No. of scholarships: Varies

Website: https://tmcf.org/our-scholarships

Requirements:

- U.S. citizen or legal resident
- Full-time undergraduate student (juniors and seniors only) enrolled at one of TMCF's 47 HBCU member schools
- Majoring in S.T.E.M., Supply Chain Management, Finance or Sales
- Minimum 3.0 GPA
- Demonstrated leadership qualities and community service experience

B. Davis Scholarship

Deadline: May 24

Award Amount: $1,000

No. of scholarships: 1

Website:
http://www.studentawardsearch.com/scholarships.htm

Requirements: High school junior or senior;
                     undergraduate college student

Café' Bustelo El Café' Del Futuro Scholarship

Deadline: May 25

Award Amount: $5,000

No. of scholarships: Varies

Website: http://www.hacu.net/hacu/scholarships.asp

Requirements:

- Hispanic heritage student
- Full-time undergraduate or graduate student
- Enrolled a four-year HACU-member institution within the U.S. or Puerto Rico

Kia Motors America, Inc. Scholarship

Deadline: May 25

Award Amount: $4,000

No. of scholarships: Varies

Website: http://www.hacu.net/hacu/scholarships.asp

Requirements:

- Hispanic heritage student
- Full-time sophomore, junior or graduate student

- Enrolled at a four-year HACU-member institution
- Minimum 3.0 GPA

AbbVie Cystic Fibrosis (CF) Scholarship

Deadline: May 27

Award Amount: $2,500 to $23,000

No. of scholarships: 40

Website: http://www.abbviecfscholarship.com

Requirements:

- Individuals who have CF only
- High school senior, undergraduate student or graduate student at master's level
- Currently enrolled or admitted to an undergraduate or graduate program for the coming fall semester

Montesi Scholarship

Deadline: May 30

Award Amount: $2,500

No. of scholarships: 1

Website:
https://www.gkbm.com/montesi-scholarship/

Requirements: Current college student or recent college graduate (within one year)

Bonnie Tiegel Memorial Scholarship Program
Deadline: May 31

Award Amount: $2,500

No. of scholarships: 1

Website:
https://www.scholarsapply.org/tiegelmemorial/

Requirements:

- High school senior (at least 17 years of age) or graduates, OR current postsecondary undergraduates who plan to enroll in full-time undergraduate study
- Attending or will attend an accredited two-year or four-year college or university for the upcoming academic year
- Pursuing a degree in broadcast journalism, communications, or journalism

Leavitt Machinery Scholarship
Deadline: May 31

Award Amount: $500

No. of scholarships: 1

Website:
http://www.forklifttrainingvancouver.com/training.php

Requirements:

- U.S. or Canadian resident attending school in the U.S. or Canada
- Currently enrolled in two-year or four-year institution
- Minimum 3.0 GPA

Liaison's Data-Inspired Future Scholarships

Deadline: May 31

Award Amount: $5,000

No. of scholarships: 1

Website: https://www.liaison.com/scholarship/

Requirements:

- U.S. or Canadian citizen or legal permanent resident
- High school senior or college student (undergraduate or graduate school)
- Enrolled in a U.S. or Canadian college, university or technical school

Michael Yasick ADHD Scholarship

Deadline: May 31

Award Amount: $2,000

No. of scholarships: 50

Website:
http://www.shireadhdscholarship.com/us/rules.aspx

Requirements:

- U.S. citizen or legal resident
- Undergraduate student accepted to or enrolled in a 2- or 4-year undergraduate program at an accredited college, university, trade school, technical school or vocational school in the U.S.
- Must be diagnosed with ADHD and under the care of a licensed health care provider for ADHD at the time application is submitted

Peck Law Firm Scholarship

Deadline: May 31

Award Amount: $2,000

No. of scholarships: 1

Website:
https://thepeckfirm.com/peck-law-firm-scholarship/

Requirements:

- U.S. citizen
- High school senior or undergraduate student
- Graduated from high school before July 1, 2019
- Minimum 3.0 GPA

Schwarzman Scholars Program

Deadline: May 31

Award Amount: $3,500 stipend, tuition, room and board, travel to/from Beijing, China, laptop, books and supplies

No. of scholarships: Up to 200 worldwide

Website:
https://www.schwarzmanscholars.org/admissions/application/

Requirements:

- Undergraduate degree completed by August 1
- Age between 18 and 29
- English language proficiency

JUNE

180 Medical Scholarship Program

Deadline: June 1

Award Amount: $1,000

No. of scholarships: 7

Website:
http://www.180medical.com/scholarships

Requirements:

- Must be under a physician's care for a spinal cord injury, spina bifida, transverse myelitis, neurogenic bladder, or ostomy (ileostomy, colostomy, or urostomy)
- U.S. citizen or legal resident
- Attending a two-year, four-year, or graduate school program full time in the upcoming fall semester

Betty Rendel Scholarship (National Federation of Republican Women)

Deadline: June 1

Award Amount: $1,000

No. of scholarships: 3

Website:
https://www.nfrw.org/rendel

Requirements: Female undergraduate majoring in political science, government or economics who has successfully completed at least two years of college coursework

Fundera College Scholarship for Student Entrepreneurs

Deadline: June 1

Award Amount: $2,000

No. of scholarships: 1

Website:
https://www.fundera.com/resources/fundera-scholarship

Requirements:

- Current or incoming college student
- Enrolled at a university in the U.S. and able to provide documentation to confirm enrollment

Galactic Unite Bytheway/UNCF Scholarship

Deadline: June 1

Award Amount: $7,500 per academic year (renewable)

No. of scholarships: Varies

Website: http://www.uncf.org

Requirements:

- Female
- High school senior
- U.S. Citizen
- Attending an accredited four-year college or university in the U.S.
- Minimum 3.2 GPA
- S.T.E.M. Majors (aeronautical engineering, aerospace engineering, astronomy, astrophysics, atmospheric physics, chemical engineering, electrical engineering, mechanical engineering, physics, robotics)

National Pathfinder Scholarship (National Federation of Republican Women)

Deadline: June 1

Award Amount: $2,500

No. of scholarships: 3

Website: https://www.nfrw.org/pathfinder

Requirements: Female undergraduate sophomore, junior and senior, as well as student enrolled in a master's degree program

Thumbtack Pro Scholarship

Deadline: June 1

Award Amount: $2,500

No. of scholarships: Varies

Website: https://www.thumbtack.com/scholarship/

Requirements:

- 18 years of age or older
- U.S. citizen or legal resident
- Currently enrolled in an undergraduate, graduate or vocational program
- Enrolled at an accredited career college, technical school, or two- or four-year college or university in the U.S.
- Pursuing a degree that enables you or others in your community to learn a new trade, develop skills, or start a small business

Vape Craft Inc. Scholarship

Deadline: June 1

Award Amount: $4,000

No. of scholarships: 1

Website: https://vapecraftinc.com/scholarships

Requirements:

- Age 18 or older
- Currently enrolled at a college or university
- In good standing, demonstrating academic excellence
- Minimum 2.8 GPA

Arctic Physical Therapy Scholarship

Deadline: June 2

Award Amount: $500

No. of scholarships: Varies

Website:
http://www.arcticchiropracticfairbanks.com/chiropractor_fair
banks.php

Requirements:

- Resident of the U.S. or Canada
- Undergraduate student enrolled full-time or part-time at an accredited college or university
- Minimum 3.0 GPA

Got A Spine Scholarship

Deadline: June 2

Award Amount: $500

No. of scholarships: 1

Website:
http://www.arcticchiropracticfairbanks.com/chiropractor_fair
banks.php

Requirements:

- U.S. or Canadian citizen
- High school senior or older
- Must plan to attend college full time by October
- Minimum 2.5 GPA

Jane Austen Society of North America Essay Contest

Deadline: June 3

Award Amount: $250 to $1,000

No. of scholarships: 3

Website: http://jasna.org/essaycontest/index.html

Requirements: Open to full-time students worldwide
                      at the high school, undergraduate or
                      graduate levels

Strada Education Network Scholarship (Thurgood Marshall College Fund)

Deadline: June 4

Award Amount: $6,200

No. of scholarships: Varies

Website: https://tmcf.org/our-scholarships

Requirements:

- U.S. citizen or legal resident
- Full-time undergraduate student enrolled at one of TMCF's 47 HBCU member schools
- Minimum 3.0 GPA
- Demonstrated leadership qualities and community service experience

Abbott & Fenner Business Consultants Scholarship
Deadline: June 14

Award Amount: $1,000

No. of scholarships: 1

Website:
http://www.abbottandfenner.com/scholarships.htm

Requirements: High school junior or senior; college/university student at accredited institutions

Helen Lansdowne Resor Scholarship
Deadline: June 14

Award Amount: $10,000

No. of scholarships: 5

Website: http://www.jwt.com/en/hlrscholarship

Requirements:

- Female student
- Registered at an undergraduate, graduate, and/or portfolio school
- Interested in a career in the advertising field

Women Forward in Technology Scholarship Program

Deadline: June 15

Award Amount: $3,000

No. of scholarships: 3

Website:
https://www.distilnetworks.com/women-forward-in-technology-scholarship/

Requirements:

- Female students only
- Enrolled or enrolling as an undergraduate or graduate student
- Attending an accredited university in the U.S.
- Minimum 3.5 GPA
- Majoring in S.T.E.M.

Comcast NBCUniversal/UNCF Scholarship

Deadline: June 16

Award Amount: Up to $5,000

No. of scholarships: 10

Website: http://www.uncf.org

Requirements:

- U.S. citizen, U.S. national, or permanent resident
- Rising college sophomore or junior
- Enrolled at an HBCU
- Minimum 3.0 GPA

TMCF/McDonald's Inspiration Celebration Scholarship

Deadline: June 17

Award Amount: $10,000

No. of scholarships: Varies

Website: http://www.tmcf.org

Requirements:

- Age 18 or older
- Attending a Historically Black College or University (HBCU)
- Minimum 3.0 GPA
- Demonstrated financial need
- Demonstrated involvement in music performance and/or education through a relevant music major and/or participation in band or similar musical activity

UNCF/Koch Scholars Program

Deadline: June 17

Award Amount: Up to $5,000

No. of scholarships: 200

Website: http://www.uncf.org

Requirements:

- African American
- U.S. citizen, permanent resident or foreign national
- High school senior
- Applying to or admitted to an eligible full-time four-year college or university. See website for list of eligible colleges/universities.
- Minimum 3.0 GPA
- Majoring in accounting, business, economics, engineering, history, philosophy or political science

Jim Dodson Law Scholarship
Deadline: June 20

Award Amount: $1,000

No. of scholarships: 1

Website:
http://www.jimdodsonlaw.com/library/the-jim-dodson-law-scholarship.cfm

Requirements:

- Full-time or part-time undergraduate student
- Enrolled in a four-year college in the U.S.
- Successfully completed 12 credit hours of college courses
- Minimum 2.75 GPA

Ricoh USA, Inc. Scholarship
Deadline: June 29

Award Amount: $2,500

No. of scholarships: Varies

Website: www.uncf.org

Requirements:

- U.S. citizen, U.S. national, or permanent resident
- College junior
- Enrolled at an HBCU
- Minimum 2.5 GPA
- Majoring in accounting, business, computer engineering, computer science, finance, information technology, marketing or mechanical engineering

True & Co: The Future Is Female Scholarship
Deadline: June 29

Award Amount: $3,000

No. of scholarships: 1

Website: https://trueandco.com/scholarship

Requirements:

- Female students only
- U. S. citizen or legal resident
- Enrolled or enrolling in U.S. college or university
- Minimum 3.0 GPA

Akash Kuruvilla Memorial Scholarship Fund
Deadline: June 30

Award Amount: $1,000

No. of scholarships: 3

Website: https://akmscholarship.com

Requirements:

- High school senior or undergraduate student at accredited college/university
- Minimum 3.5 GPA for high school student; minimum 3.0 GPA for college student
- Demonstrate financial need

AlgaeCal Health Scholarship
Deadline: June 30

Award Amount: $1,000

No. of scholarships: 1

Website:
https://www.algaecal.com/expert-insights/algaecal-scholarships/

Requirements:

- College student attending a post-secondary institute in the U.S. or Canada
- Minimum 3.0 GPA

Americanism Educational Leaders Essay Contest
Deadline: June 30

Award Amount: $1,000 to $2,500

No. of scholarships: 3

Website:
http://infoguides.pepperdine.edu/AEL

Requirements:

- U.S. citizen
- Undergraduate student at an accredited four-year U.S. college or university

Digital Privacy Scholarship

Deadline: June 30

Award Amount: $500 to $1,500

No. of scholarships: 2

Website:
http://www.digitalresponsibility.org/scholarships/

Requirements:

- U.S. citizen or legal resident
- High school student, undergraduate or graduate college student

Frank and Brennie Morgan Prize for Outstanding Research in Mathematics (Mathematical Association of America)

Deadline: June 30

Award Amount: $1,200

No. of scholarships: Varies

Website:
http://www.maa.org/programs/maa-awards/research-awards/morgan-prize/morgan-prize-information

Requirements:

- Undergraduate student at a college or university in Canada, Mexico or the United States
- Individual or students working jointly demonstrating outstanding research in mathematics

Hylan Family Scholarship

Deadline: June 30

Award Amount: $2,500.

No. of scholarships: 1

Website: https://www.drbradhylan.com/scholarship.html

Requirements:

- High school senior or current college student
- Attending college at an accredited community college, online college, or university in upcoming fall semester

Key Thinkers Scholarship

Deadline: June 30

Award Amount: $2,500

No. of scholarships: 1

Website: https://www.moneykey.com/scholarship/

Requirements:

- U.S. citizen or permanent resident
- 18 years or older

- Enrolled as a full-time student at an accredited college, university, or trade school in the U.S.
- Minimum 3.0 GPA

OppU Achievers Scholarship

Deadline: June 30

Award Amount: $2,500

No. of scholarships: 1

Website: https://www.opploans.com/scholarship/

Requirements:

- U. S. citizen
- Enrolled full-time in high school or at least part-time in college, graduate, professional, or trade school
- Minimum 3.0 GPA

Writers' Square, Hakka Foundation Essay Contest

Deadline: June 30

Award Amount: $100 to $1,000

No. of scholarships: 15

Website: http://www.writerssquare.org/rules-en

Requirements:

- Division 1: Grades 1-6 (any student enrolled in school)
- Division 2: Grades7-12 (any student enrolled in school)
- Division 3: College (any student enrolled in college)

JULY

Coastal Scholarship

Deadline: July 1

Award Amount: $5,000

No. of scholarships: 1

Website:
https://www.coastal.com/scholarships/2018

Requirements:

- Undergraduate student in the U.S.
- Enrolled at an accredited college or university
- Minimum 3.3 GPA

Joseph J. LoRusso College Scholarship

Deadline: July 1

Award Amount: $1,000

No. of scholarships: 1

Website: https://injuryflorida.lawyer/scholarship/

Requirements:

- High school senior or current college student
- Attending an accredited U.S. college or university in fall of upcoming academic year

KB Delta Compressor Valve Parts Scholarship

Deadline: July 1

Award Amount: $1,000

No. of scholarships: 1

Website: http://kbdelta.com/scholarship.html

Requirements: Student enrolled in any accredited college or university

Store Coach's Entrepreneur Scholarship
Deadline: July 1

Award Amount: $1,000

No. of scholarships: 1

Website:
https://storecoach.com/coachs-ecommerce-entrepreneur-scholarship

Requirements:

- Full- or part-time college student currently enrolled for the upcoming semester
- Interested in online businesses

Goedeker's College Scholarship
Deadline: July 7

Award Amount: $100 to $500

No. of scholarships: 3

Website:
http://www.goedekers.com/college-scholarship

Requirements:

- Accepted or enrolled in accredited college/university
- Minimum 3.0 GPA

Weary Scholarship

Deadline: July 13

Award Amount: $3,000

No. of scholarships: Varies

Website:
https://www.midamericacabletv.com/weary-scholarship/

Requirements:

- Cable industry employees, their spouses and children in the Mid-America region ONLY
- Reside in one of the qualifying states: AR, IL, IA, KS, MO, NE, OK or TX
- Minimum 2.8 GPA (high school and/or college)

Resume Companion Scholarship

Deadline: July 14

Award Amount: $1,000

No. of scholarships: 1

Website:
http://resumecompanion.com/scholarship

Requirements: Enrolled, or due to be enrolled, in full-time university education for the semester for which they are applying

Creative Safety Supply Scholarship

Deadline: July 15

Award Amount: $1,000

No. of scholarships: 1

Website:
https://www.creativesafetysupply.com/scholarship/

Requirements:

- U.S. citizen or permanent resident
- Enrolled in a college, university, or vocational school for the upcoming term
- Minimum 3.0 GPA

DirectTextbook.com Scholarship Essay Contest

Deadline: July 15

Award Amount: $250 to $2,500

No. of scholarships: 3

Website:
http://www.directtextbook.com/scholarship.php

Requirements:

- U.S. citizen or legal resident
- Undergraduate student enrolled in an accredited two- or four-year college/university
- Minimum 2.0 GPA
- Must not be currently incarcerated

Duffy Law Scholarship
Deadline: July 15

Award Amount: $1,000

No. of scholarships: 1

Website:
http://www.duffylawct.com/duffy-law-llc-1000-scholarship/

Requirements:

- Currently attending or have been accepted at an accredited American college or university
- Full-time undergraduate, graduate student, or law student

BankMobile Financial Empowerment Scholarship
Deadline: July 19

Award Amount: $1,500

No. of scholarships: 1

Website:
https://www.bankmobile.com/the-annual-bankmobile-financial-literacy-scholarship/

Requirements:

- U.S. citizen
- Attend or accepted to an accredited college or university
- Minimum 3.0 GPA

Panda Cares/UNCF Scholars Program

Deadline: July 20

Award Amount: Up to $10,000

No. of scholarships: 400

Website: http://www.uncf.org

Requirements:

- U.S. citizen, national, or permanent resident
- High school senior
- Enrolled full-time at an accredited U.S. four-year college or university in upcoming fall semester
- Minimum 2.8 GPA
- Demonstrate financial need and Pell Grant eligible
- Reside in one of the following states: AK, AZ, AR, CA, CO, FL, GA, HI, ID, IL, IN, IA, KS, MD, MI, MN, MO, NE, NV, NJ, NM, NY, OK, OR, PA, PR, TN, TX, UT, VA, WA, WI

NASCAR Wendell Scott Sr/UNCF Scholarship

Deadline: July 25

Award Amount: Up to $10,000

No. of scholarships: Varies

Website: http://www.uncf.org

Requirements:

- U.S. citizen, national, or permanent resident
- Minority student
- Undergraduate or graduate student
- Enrolled full-time at a four-year college or university

- Minimum 3.0 GPA
- Majoring in a business-related discipline, communications, engineering, information technology or public relations

Delta Airlines New York/UNCF Scholarship
Deadline: July 27

Award Amount: Up to $4,400

No. of scholarships: Varies

Website: http://www.uncf.org

Requirements:

- U.S. citizen, national, or permanent resident
- Resident of state of New York
- Undergraduate student
- Enrolled at an accredited four-year U.S. college or university
- Minimum 2.5 GPA
- Demonstrate unmet financial need

Bachus & Schanker, LLC Scholarship
Deadline: July 30

Award Amount: $2,000

No. of scholarships: 1

Website: http://www.coloradolaw.net/scholarship/

Requirements:

- High school senior or undergraduate student
- Accepted to or attending a four-year university
- Minimum 3.0 GPA

CardRates.com Financial Futures Scholarship

Deadline: July 30

Award Amount: $1,000

No. of scholarships: 1

Website: https://www.cardrates.com/scholarship/

Requirements:

- U.S. resident
- High school senior or current college student
- Minimum 3.5 GPA
- Majoring in business, accounting, finance, mathematics, management, and others related to the personal finance industry

Abrahamson & Uiterwyk Scholarship

Deadline: July 31

Award Amount: $1,500

No. of scholarships: 1

Website:
http://www.theinjurylawyers.com/scholarship/

Requirements:

- U.S. resident
- Current high school senior OR current college student

Apex Minecraft Scholarship

Deadline: July 31

Award Amount: $2,000

No. of scholarships: 1

Website:
https://apexminecrafthosting.com/minecraft-scholarship/

Requirements:

- U.S. citizen
- Enrolled in high school or college
- Minimum 3.0 GPA

From Failure to Promise Essay Contest
Deadline: July 31

Award Amount: $10,000 (with three [3] $500
                      honorable mentions)

No. of scholarships: 4 total (see above)

Website:
http://www.fromfailuretopromise.com/essay-scholarship-contest--html

Requirements:

- High school senior, undergraduate or graduate student
- Pursuing a degree at an accredited college or university in the U.S. or Canada
- Minimum 2.5 GPA

Gen and Kelly Tanabe Scholarship
Deadline: July 31

Award Amount: $1,000

No. of scholarships: 3

Website: http://www.genkellyscholarship.com

Requirements:

- U.S. citizen or legal resident
- High school student from 9th to 12th grade OR undergraduate or graduate college student

The Law Offices of Hovanes Margarian Scholarship
Deadline: July 31

Award Amount: $1,000

No. of scholarships: 5

Website:
http://www.margarianlaw.com/scholarship

Requirements:

- High school junior or senior, undergraduate and graduate college student
- Demonstrate financial need
- Demonstrate commitment to heritage, community and society

Platt Family Scholarship Prize Essay Contest
Deadline: July 31

Award Amount: $500 to $1,500

No. of scholarships: 3

Website:
http://www.thelincolnforum.org/scholarship-essay-contest

Requirements: Full time, undergraduate student enrolled in an American college or university

Quit Smoking Scholarship

Deadline: July 31

Award Amount: $5,000

No. of scholarships: 3

Website:
https://ecigarettereviewed.com/scholarship/

Requirements:

- 14 years or order
- Accepted to or enrolled in a high school, college or university in the U.S.

Redfin Scholarship

Deadline: July 31

Award Amount: $2,500

No. of scholarships: 1

Website:
https://www.redfin.com/resources/scholarship

Requirements:

- Legal U.S. resident
- Graduating high school senior or current freshman, sophomore, or junior in college attending an accredited university or college
- Minimum 3.5 GPA

Self Lender Scholarship

Deadline: July 31

Award Amount: $1,000

No. of scholarships: 1

Website: https://www.selflender.com/scholarship

Requirements:

- Full-time undergraduate or graduate student
- Enrolled at a two- or four-year university
- Majoring in one of the following: Business, finance, entrepreneurship, computer science, economics, accounting or mathematics

Wine Country Gift Baskets Spirit of Giving Scholarship

Deadline: July 31

Award Amount: $1,000

No. of scholarships: 3

Website: https://scholarship-positions.com/wine-country-gift-baskets-spirit-of-giving-scholarship/2018/08/16/

Requirements:

- High school senior or current college student
- Planning to attend college or another form of post-secondary education full-time in the coming academic year
- Not an employee or family member of Wine Country Gift Baskets

AUGUST

Nurses Make a Difference Scholarship
Deadline: August 1

Award Amount: $1,000

No. of scholarships: 1

Website:
http://www.cascadehealthcaresolutions.com/Chs_scholarship
_a/364.htm

Requirements:

- U.S. citizen or legal resident
- High school senior accepted into college and plan to study nursing, or undergraduate student pursuing a nursing degree program at an accredited college/university
- Minimum 3.0 GPA
- Majoring in nursing

Patsy Takemoto Mink Education Foundation Scholarship
Deadline: August 1

Award Amount: Up to $5,000

No. of scholarships: 5

Website: http://www.patsyminkfoundation.org

Requirements:

- U. S. citizen
- Female
- Age 17 or order
- Mother, with minor children

- Enrolled in a skills training, ESL or GED program; or pursuing a technical/vocational degree, an associate's degree, a first bachelor's degree, or a graduate degree
- Low-income family household with annual income less than $17,500 for a family of 2; $22,000 for a family of 3; $26,500 for a family of 4

SingleCare Medical Scholarship

Deadline: August 1

Award Amount: $1,000

No. of scholarships: 3

Website: https://www.singlecare.com/scholarship

Requirements:

- Currently enrolled or planning to enroll in a medical program in the upcoming semester
- Attending an accredited medical school program, pharmacy school program, or nursing school program in the U.S.

Devconhomesecurity Scholarship

Deadline: August 15

Award Amount: $2,500

No. of scholarships: 1

Website:
http://devconhomesecurity.com/scholarship

Requirements:

- U.S. citizen or permanent resident
- At least 18 years old

- Full-time undergraduate or graduate student attending a college or university in the U.S.
- Minimum 3.0 GPA

Hackard Law Scholarship

Deadline: August 15

Award Amount: $2,500

No. of scholarships: 1

Website:
https://www.hackardlaw.com/Academic-Scholarship.shtml

Requirements:

- 18 years of age or older
- Enrolled as a student in a U.S. college or university
- U.S. citizen
- In good academic standing with higher educational institution at which student is enrolled

Social Network Elite Instagram Growth Scholarship

Deadline: August 15

Award Amount: $1,000

No. of scholarships: 1

Website:
https://www.socialnetworkelite.com/scholarship

Requirements:

- Enrolled in any accredited college program in the upcoming fall semester
- Minimum 3.7 GPA
- Majoring in business

Procter & Gamble/UNCF General Scholarship

Deadline: August 20

Award Amount: Up to $5,000

No. of scholarships: Varies

Website: http://www.uncf.org

Requirements:

- U.S. citizen, U.S. national, or permanent resident
- High school senior or undergraduate student
- Enrolled at any accredited four-year college or university within the U.S.
- Minimum 3.0 GPA
- Majoring in business, information technology or public relations

Procter & Gamble/UNCF STEM Scholarship

Deadline: August 20

Award Amount: Up to $5,000

No. of scholarships: Varies

Website: http://www.uncf.org

Requirements:

- U.S. citizen, U.S. national, or permanent resident
- High school senior or undergraduate student
- Enrolled at any accredited four-year college or university within the U.S.
- Minimum 3.0 GPA
- Majoring in S.T.E.M.-related field

Wikibuy eCommerce and Online Retail Scholarship

Deadline: August 21

Award Amount: $2,500

No. of scholarships: 1

Website: https://wikibuy.com/scholarship

Requirements:

- Undergraduate student attending an accredited U.S. two-or four-year college or university
- Minimum 3.4 GPA
- Major or minor in business administration and management, business (general), finance, accounting, or other related business degrees

DialMyCalls.com Scholarship

Deadline: August 22

Award Amount: $500

No. of scholarships: 2

Website:
http://www.dialmycalls.com/scholarship.html

Requirements:

- U.S. citizen or legal resident
- Currently enrolled in accredited two- or four-year college/university
- Minimum 2.0 GPA
- Not currently incarcerated

CoffeeForLess.com "Hit the Books" Scholarship

Deadline: August 25

Award Amount: $500

No. of scholarships: 1

Website:
http://www.coffeeforless.com/scholarship

Requirements:

- Age 18 to 25
- Enrolled in accredited college/university

The Financial Sumo Educational Scholarship Program

Deadline: August 29

Award Amount: $1,000

No. of scholarships: 1

Website:
http://www.financialsumo.com/scholarship/

Requirement: Any student currently attending an
accredited college

Clubs of America Scholarship

Deadline: August 31

Award Amount: $1,500

No. of scholarships: 1

Website:
http://www.greatclubs.com/scholarship-award-for-career-success.asp

Requirements:

- Undergraduate student at accredited college/university
- Minimum 3.0 GPA

Greg Baumgartner Scholarship

Deadline: August 31

Award Amount: $1,000

No. of scholarships: 1

Website:
http://www.texas-truckaccidentlawyer.com/scholarship/greg-baumgartner-scholarship/

Requirements:

- Targets students who pay their way through school without parental assistance
- Enrolled in high school or college in the U.S.
- Minimum 3.0 GPA

iVein Health & Wellness Scholarship

Deadline: August 31

Award Amount: $2,500

No. of scholarships: 1

Website: https://www.ivein.com/scholarship/

Requirements:

- Current full-time undergraduate/graduate student
- Attending an accredited U.S. university or college
- Minimum 3.4 GPA

OklahomaLawyer.com Annual Scholarship

Deadline: August 31

Award Amount: $1,000

No. of scholarships: 1

Website: http://oklahomalawyer.com/scholarship/

Requirements:

- U.S. citizen living in the U.S. and attending school in the U.S.
- High school senior or college student

CHAPTER 11

PURSUE PAID INTERNSHIPS

As mentioned in Chapter 8, internships provide another avenue to earn much-needed funds for college. While some internships offer only course credit and do not provide monetary compensation, many of them include paid stipends, housing, and even salaries.

An internship for course credit offers needed exposure within the student's field of study, but a paid internship offers both the exposure and monetary rewards. A paid internship can provide much-needed funds for college expenses throughout the semester or academic year. Since the funds go directly to the student, they can be used for books, housing, transportation, clothing, laptops, and other expenses directly related to the student's college matriculation.

Internships can be available during the summer or during the academic year, usually for either the fall or spring semester. They are usually offered to college students during their junior and/or senior years once their course curriculum is more directly related to their chosen major or field of study. Some are also offered to graduate students in master's or doctoral programs and to students in law school or medical school. Being able to list an internship with a major corporation can go a long way toward favorable results in the scholarship award process and also for full-time employment after graduation.

The college or university the student attends is a good source for available internship opportunities. Check with the institution's career office or the academic advisor.

Following are some paid internships students may pursue:

Deloitte Internship
Website:
https://www2.deloitte.com/us/en/pages/careers/articles/join-deloitte-undergraduate-degree-opportunities.html

Requirements:

- High academic achievement
- Majoring in accounting or finance
- College undergraduate or graduate student

El Paso Electric Internship
Website:
https://www.epelectric.com/careers/summer-college-internship-program

Requirements:

- Currently enrolled full-time as an undergraduate or graduate student
- Enrolled at an accredited college or university in the U.S. and completed at least two (2) semesters
- Minimum 3.0 GPA and in good academic standing
- Pursuing an undergraduate or graduate degree in science, math, engineering, accounting, finance, business or related field
- Legally authorized to work in the U.S.

ESPN Internship
Website:
https://espncareers.com/college/internships

Locations: Bristol, VA; New York, NY; Austin, TX; Charlotte, NC; and Los Angeles, CA

Requirements:

- Currently enrolled in a degree program at the time of application
- Authorized to work for any U.S.-based employer upon graduation

Federal Deposit Insurance Corporation (FDIC) Summer Legal Intern Program
Website: https://www.fdic.gov/about/legalinterns

Locations: Washington, DC and Arlington, VA

Requirements:

- Currently enrolled in an accredited Juris Doctorate (JD) or LL.M program
- Completion of one full academic year of graduate level education OR eligibility under the Superior Academic Achievement Provision and completion of a bachelor's degree
- Minimum 2.5 GPA and remain in good academic standing

Hershey Entertainment & Resorts Internship

Website: https://www.hersheyjobs.com

Requirements:

- Possess strong communication skills
- Exhibit enthusiasm, professionalism, and a personal drive for success
- Interest in hospitality or tourism profession

Marsh & McLennan Companies Internship

Website: https://careers.mmc.com

Location: Washington, DC

Requirements:

- Rising college junior or senior
- Working toward a B.A. or a B.S. in any major
- High academic achievement
- Demonstrate exceptional analytical and critical thinking skills
- Coursework and/or experience in finance, economics, accounting, statistical analysis/econometrics, and computer programming preferred

National Air and Space Museum Summer Internship Program

Website:
https://airandspace.si.edu/support/get-involved/internships

Location: Washington, DC

Requirements: College student majoring in any field of study

Paypal Internship
Website: https://www.uncf.org

Requirements:

- U.S. citizen
- Ethnic minority
- College sophomore, junior, senior, 5th year senior, master's student, or doctoral student
- Majoring in computer science, engineering, information technology, risk management
- Experience in Java and Java Script programming languages

Price Waterhouse Coopers Internship
Website:
https://www.pwc.com/us/en/careers/entry-level/programs-events/start.html

Requirements:

- Ethnic minority
- College sophomore in a 4-year program, or a college sophomore or junior in a 5-year program
- Minimum 3.3 GPA
- Pursuing a bachelor's degree in accounting or a STEM major

CHAPTER 12

DEVELOP YOUR POST-AWARD STRATEGY

Once your scholarship awards start rolling in, you may believe your work is done. However, there are still a variety of tasks that are required to complete the scholarship process.

First, you should promptly return any forms that need to be completed and signed. Most scholarship awards have to be accepted in writing for the process to be finalized.

Second, be sure to formally thank the organization that awarded the scholarship. This should be done either with a formal letter through snail mail or a formal email. Informal communication for this purpose should be avoided, including text messages, phone calls, or impromptu email messages that are not professionally structured. You will want the sponsoring organization to have an official record of your statement of gratitude.

Some scholarship organizations may request that you submit thank you letters to their sponsors, or that you complete surveys about the scholarship experience or your educational achievements. Be sure to comply with all requests.

Third, maintain copies of all formal award documents in a file, including the award letter and any supporting documentation. If you used a filing system while performing your scholarship research, you may include the information in the same file used to retain the application information.

These items will likely be needed later to send to the educational institution's financial aid or admissions department. The arrival of funds often does not occur until after the next semester commences, or even later, and the documentation will serve as proof that arrival of the funds is imminent.

Fourth, keep track of each scholarship and the amount awarded in a spreadsheet program, like Excel. Tabulate the total amount received to ensure that your records correspond with those maintained by the college/university.

Fifth, add the scholarship(s) you received to the "Honors and Awards" section of your resume. Being a scholarship recipient offers a certain level of prestige, one that will be noticed by future employers and other key decision makers.

In fact, as your list of scholarship awards expands you will be afforded other promising career opportunities, such as internships and inclusion in leadership conferences. These opportunities will not only provide additional college funds but set you apart from other college graduates when you submit applications for professional career positions.

Next, review the information for all of the scholarships for which you submitted applications to determine which ones you can submit applications to for the following academic year. For those scholarships that sent you letters of regret, do not let the fact that you did not receive the scholarship the first time deter you from applying in the future. Often, the second time around will reap some rewards simply because you are already familiar with the process. A second application should be superior to the first, and you might receive a positive response the second time around.

In addition, some of the awards you receive may be renewable annually. Some may automatically renew if you meet certain criteria, such as a minimum grade point average and continued enrollment in a four-year institution. Maintaining the information about both types of scholarships separately will help you to keep track of re-submissions for the coming years.

Continue to research and pursue scholarship opportunities, even after you have reached your goal and received awards to cover your expenses. According to the College Board, the cost of college tuition is increasing annually at the rate of 3 percent.[22] It is a near certainty that your funding needs will increase from year to year, so it is best to be prepared for this likely occurrence.

Finally, share the information you have learned with others who desire to attend college debt-free. When students graduate with zero or minimal debt, the overall health of the American economy is strengthened. Those students will be able to purchase homes, automobiles, and other major items, and build savings accounts much sooner without the proverbial albatross of monthly student loan payments around their necks. They will not have the constant pressure of a seemingly never-ending balance due because most of their student loan payments go toward interest, not the principal. That is the ultimate purpose of this book: To help thousands of students across America and the world to obtain a debt-free college education.

ABOUT THE AUTHOR

Gwen Richardson has been a writer and editor for more than 25 years. Her commentaries have appeared in several daily newspapers, including the *Houston Chronicle, Detroit Free Press, Dallas Morning News* and *Philadelphia Inquirer.*

As her daughter's college years approached, she began researching scholarship opportunities and became passionate about the issue of college loan debt. As a result, her daughter attended all four years at an out-of-state college and graduated with zero college loan debt. Ms. Richardson's passion led to a desire to champion the cause of a debt-free college education for students across the United States, and she is a frequent speaker to youth groups on the subject of scholarships and college loans. *101 Scholarship Applications* was nominated for a 2015 NAACP Image Award. This book was originally published in 2014 and a revised edition is published in January of each year.

A long-time entrepreneur and a graduate of Georgetown University, Ms. Richardson currently resides in Houston, Texas. Communication via email is welcome, including speaking requests. Email the author at gwenrichardson123@gmail.com.

Visit the author's website: www.gwenrichardson.com

Alphabetical Index of Scholarships and Internships

Gwen Richardson

OTHER BOOKS BY GWEN RICHARDSON
(Kindle version also available)

The Genesis Files is a fast-paced mystery based in Houston, Texas. The main character is a journalist, Lloyd Palmer, who meets a mysterious stranger while interviewing potential witnesses to a murder-suicide. This chance meeting leads Lloyd down a path which changes his life, but his journey is fraught with peril, as both he and his family barely escape a hired assassin. 312 pp. $15.00

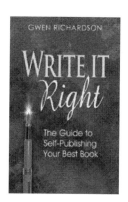

Write It Right: The Guide to Self-Publishing Your Best Book provides both aspiring and seasoned authors with a road map to success. 142 pp. $12.00

You Are Wonderfully Made: 12 Life-Changing Principles for Teen Girls to Embrace empowers teen girls with the tools they need to successfully navigate their teen years and avoid the pitfalls that can derail their futures. They can be adopted by any teen girl, regardless of her family background, economic status, ethnicity, or educational achievement level. 94 pp. $10.00

21 of Satan's Schemes, Tricks and Devices describes twenty-one of Satan's schemes, tricks, and devices; however, this list is not, by any means, all-inclusive. Satan's schemes are designed to lead us into sin and keep us mired there. Moreover, in utilizing his tricks, his intentions are to render us ineffective in our own faith walk as well as in leading others to Christ. 101 pp. $12.00

Autographed copies of all titles by Gwen Richardson can be ordered via her web site: www.gwenrichardson.com

Copies can also be ordered by calling Cushcity Communications at its toll-free number: 1-800-340-5454

Other online sources for purchase: www.amazon.com and www.createspace.com

END NOTES

[1] Harvard University website, https://www.harvard.edu/about-harvard/harvard-glance, Accessed Nov. 8, 2017.

[2] Lisa Kiplinger, "Ack! $37,000 in college debt! Now what? Top tips from 2 authors," June 9, 2016, *USA Today*, www.usatoday.com, Accessed June 9, 2016.

[3] Zack Friedman, "Student Loan Debt In 2017: A $1.3 Trillion Crisis," Feb. 21, 2017, *Forbes*, www.forbes.com, Accessed Dec. 21, 2017.

[4] Delano R. Franklin and Samuel W. Zwickel, "Record-Low 4.59 Percent of Applicants Accepted to Harvard Class of 2022," *The Harvard Crimson*, www.thecrimson.com, Accessed Dec. 6, 2018.

[5] Fifth Third Bank Scholarship Program, https://financeacademy.53.com/scholarship/, Accessed July 27, 2018.

[6] Lorena Roberts, "How to Pay Off Your Student Loans Faster," *College Campus Life News*, www.uloop.com, Accessed Jan. 4, 2018.

[7] Herrera, 2014.

[8] Andy Josuweit, "A Look at the Shocking Student Loan Debt Statistics for 2016," www.studentloanhero.com, Accessed Sept. 5, 2016.

[9] Herrera, 2014.

[10] Dell Scholars Program, http://www.dellscholarsprogram.org/scholarship/overview, Accessed Aug. 23, 2014

[11] Lynnette Khalfani Cox, "5 College Scholarship Scams to Avoid," July 21, 2014, *Ebony*, www.ebony.com, Accessed Sept. 9, 2014

[12] Internal Revenue Service, Publication 970, Tax Benefits for Education, www.irs.gov

[13] U.S. Department of Education website, https://studentaid.ed.gov/fafsa, Accessed Sept. 6, 2014

[14] Elizabeth Hoyt, "President Obama Announces Changes to 2017-2018 FAFSA," Sept. 17, 2015, Fastweb.com, http://www.fastweb.com/financial-aid/articles/President-Obama-Announces-Changes-to-2017-18-FAFSA, Accessed Sept. 23, 2015

[15] Herrera, 2014.

[16] Herrera, 2014.

[17] Elizabeth Hoyt, "Crowdfunding for college," Sept. 11, 2013, Fastweb.com, http://www.fastweb.com/financial-aid/articles/4035-crowdfunding-for-college, Accessed Sept. 5, 2014

[18] Andrew Josuweit, "5 Crowdfunding Sites That Will Destroy Your Student Loan Debt," *Forbes*, May 2, 2018, www.forbes.com, Accessed

May 2, 2018.

[19] Andrew Josuweit, 2018.

[20] Andrew Josuweit, 2018.

[21] Hoyt, 2013

[22] "Trends in Higher Education: Average Rates of Growth of Published Charges by Decade," College Board, https://trends.collegeboard.org/college-pricing/figures-tables/average-rates-growth-tuition-and-fees-over-time, Accessed Sept. 2, 2014

Made in the USA
Lexington, KY
02 November 2019